Recipes and Dreams

FROM AN ITALIAN LIFE

Recipes and Dreams

FROM AN ITALIAN LIFE

Tessa Kiros

PHOTOGRAPHY
MANOS CHATZIKONSTANTIS

STYLING
MICHAIL TOUROS

ART DIRECTION
LISA GREENBERG

Andrews McMeel
Publishing, LLC
Kansas City · Sydney · London

TO ALL OF THE
WONDERFUL MATRIARCHS I HAVE
BEEN LUCKY TO MEET.

For Yasmine & Cassia
For Wilma who gives with both hands

CONTENTS

Introduction

This book is inspired by my mother-in-law, Wilma, and the many other wonder women that roam freely about. Wilma is a shining beacon of inspiration—never missing a step while busily folding, soaking, plopping, and puffing things out of thin air. She always has the right color button or shade of Italian thread handy and a pair of scissors tied and tucked into the inside pocket of her handbag. She is chock-a-block full of herbs and recipes, energy and ideas, love and inspiration. She has knowledge of war, years gone by, acceptance, humility. And the Lord knows—no bitterness. She glides along, scooping up new ideas, armfuls of flowers and herbs, always ready to sprinkle droplets of wisdom into the air and scatter seeds over the younger if they ask—if they want. She stands back wearing her expressions and experiences well, folding them into her cakes and sauces and between the lines of her stories...

She came from a family of six children. She tells of how they had to be filled up on soups and staples that would go a long way. Filled up on stories. Her mother was a great cook. I can imagine her, just like Wilma, constantly foraging about both outside and in. She would have searched a lifetime for those natural herbs and flowers and tidbits to slip into her loved ones' palate. She would have collected endless ideas, countless cuttings and pressed them with her spring flowers between her heaviest books and into her stores. She would have been rattling in jars and drawers and boxes to pull out bits of potential, snippings from here and there that she had tucked away for one of those gray days where she would need some reaching-into-secret-places-for-inspiration and then patchworking it all together. At night Wilma would put the children to bed and spin on into the kitchen to get on with her egg-white cake or *torta campagnola* for breakfast the next morning. And when she wasn't feeling fantastic she'd tie a beautiful colored foulard around her neck she said, so people would be drawn to that.

This is an ode to the matriarchal figures in my life. Wilma and others who have inspired me with their stories and recipes. Their collectings and gatherings. Their offerings. They have sung well, and among the trousseaux they have prepared for us they have slipped in diamonds of wisdom, snippings of experience of mystery—of what to layer between our sheets, of how to hold the man down (through his stomach). They knew what was to be done, was to be done. How to make cakes people liked and splash love over the children. They knew how to roll these things off from their souls.

The trousseau, or dowry, was very common

Introduction

in Wilma's time. Passing down stories and traditions through the night. Past secrets. Recipes. Sturdy stacks of heavy oval porcelain plates and beautiful teapots. Solid casserole dishes and old silver that would carry on with candles into much of the future and mingle with lace and lavender in glowing atmospheres. There would be tips and methods to nourish this woman, passed down through her bloodline. From her mother and grandmother. The sheets would be embroidered by hand and stitched with love and memories. With experience. With the woman's initials. They were beautiful and of the finest material. Hand-picked. Handmade. Handed down with the chests. This was the woman's value. What she brought to the marriage. To the home.

While the gentleman brought his craft, his work, his money, she brought her knowledge. Her know-how. Her art. Swimming through her veins and winding through her stitching. Spilling out into her broths. The way she had been taught. Of family. Of love. Of how to keep her home. And which herbs to use. She had the time and the *voglia* for this. And the secrets. Passed down to her, from her mother, her grandmother... I love this. These stories are our birthright. We need to lean up closer and listen. To those who have grown their own vegetables and turned their toilings and scrapings into practical masterpieces. We need to sow our seeds, too, and be patient. Show up for the collecting when the time is right. Roll with it all. Wait. Breathe. How do we keep it? How do we hold it? We continue to swap. To collect and pass on. So they don't drift away and get forgotten. And we ask. We look for pretty tins and boxes to store these older morsels and jewels of information. And we walk with a step in the now, a step in the then, and try to catch glimpses of other trousseaux as we go. We fill the chests that we will one day present to others.

Here is some inspiration I have collected. The recipes are simple and practical. They cover a multitude of uses and have at their roots a nourishing, loving, and protecting clan of women. May they encourage you to pull a good roast out of the oven, stuff a chicken's neck, add an extra sugar lump, clump of herbs, peppercorns, or roses to your plates, and sway to the sounds of nature.

x Tessa

Many years ago, a mother would teach her daughter how to keep a home using a doll's house as an example. The daughter would learn how to make sense of it all and keep order through the various rooms. She would also be taught the art of hospitality, the times of year of celebration, how to decorate the house, and, eventually, how to keep order and make sense of her own home.

To make a home that looks and smells and feels like a home—with burnished pots simmering on the stovetop and candles glowing warmly among the trousseau linen hanging long from the tables. How to make the most of what the seasons give by preserving things. That bustling feeling through the days of the week with the various chores of washing, ironing, and baking, and the harmony her know-how would bring.

SAPIENTE

WORDS/PAROLE

IF YOU DROP A KNIFE, IT MEANS
A MAN IS COMING TO VISIT.
IF YOU DROP A FORK, IT MEANS
A WOMAN IS COMING.

The

LINEN
CUPBOARD

LA BIANCHERIA

One Week's Worth

—MONDAY—
*WASHING
DAY*

—TUESDAY—
*IRONING
DAY*

—WEDNESDAY—
*MENDING & SEWING
DAY*

—THURSDAY—
*MARKET
DAY*

—FRIDAY—
*CLEANING
DAY*

—SATURDAY—
*BAKING
DAY*

—SUNDAY—
*RESTING
DAY*

WILMA'S SHEETS

1 MATTRESS COVER
IN THICKER MATERIAL

1 UNDERSHEET
(IN WILMA'S DAY THEY
DIDN'T HAVE FITTED
SHEETS SO THEY WERE
EASIER TO FOLD)

1 HANDMADE TOP
SHEET EMBROIDERED
WITH INITIALS OR
EMBLEMS

2 MATCHING
EMBROIDERED TOP
PILLOWCASES

2 PLAINER
PILLOWCASES (FOR
SECOND PILLOWS)

4 PILLOW COVERS TO
PROTECT THE PILLOWS
BETTER

RIBBONS OF GENEROUS
LENGTHS—A COLOR
OR PATTERN THAT WILL
REPRESENT ALL YOUR SETS

Makes 1 double bed

Wilma first had a linen shop, so she knows about these things. How to keep sheets in order. My linen cupboard used to consist of mixed piles of tablecloths, towels, single and double sheets, mismatched pillowcases, stray socks, and everything else possible, all avalanching down on me.

This is what Wilma taught me for my linen cupboard. It's a wonderful method that's well worth a try. You may adjust the "recipe" to suit your personal tastes. It is a good idea to keep some extra cut ribbons tied on a nail on the inside door of your cupboard for when you need them.

In Wilma's day, the bedspread was generally crocheted by hand or made of satin and it would cover the bed completely, keeping the sheets free of dust.

Firstly, measure your cupboard to decide how many piles of sheets can fit on a shelf. Wilma's cupboard measures 20 inches across, so she folds her sheets to less than 10 inches so she can fit in two piles. Fold the freshly washed top sheet from top to bottom and then the other way—it should go four times. Then, turn and make one fold of about 8 inches and proceed folding up the rest like an accordion.

The finished measure is about 8 by 10 inches in this case. Fold the bottom sheet and mattress cover so they will be the same finished measure as the top sheet. Pillowcases are folded and kept on top of the pile and are usually smaller than the folded sheets. Once the mattress cover, undersheet, top sheet, and pillowcases are all in a good and compact pile, tie this bundle together neatly with the colored ribbon of your choice that should be used now for all sets, and pack into your linen cupboard. Continue with the double sets. All the bundles should sit neatly on top of one another.

Proceed in the same way for single sheet sets, but with a different color ribbon, of course. Now, when you open the cupboard, you will know at a glance what's what.

The same method can be used for towel sets, table linen, and other sets of things.

Lasts a lifetime.

SAPIENTE

WORDS/PAROLE

USE DIFFERENT COLORED RIBBONS TO TIE
UP SETS OF SINGLE AND DOUBLE SHEETS SO
YOU KNOW WHETHER YOU ARE ARTHUR OR
MARTHA WHEN YOU OPEN THE CUPBOARD.

ACQUA DI LAVANDA

2½ TABLESPOONS
LAVENDER FLOWERS,
NO STALKS

4 CUPS COLD WATER

*You can use dried or fresh flowers here. The stalks will
color your water, so use only the flowers. Put the scented
water in a spray bottle to dampen linen when ironing, for
a subtle fragrance.*

Wrap the lavender in a square of cheesecloth and tie
in a tight ball. Pour the water into a bowl and add the
lavender ball. Leave to sit for 20 to 30 minutes, removing
the lavender as soon as the water begins to change color.
Pour into a spray bottle and it will keep for a long time.

JASMINE
GARLANDS

A FEW BRANCHES OF
JASMINE

NEEDLE AND ENOUGH
THREAD

PATIENCE

Jasmine garlands can be made in summer. Using
a needle and long thread, tack stitch them together
through the base of the flowers and tie them into long
necklaces. These render a beautiful fragrance.

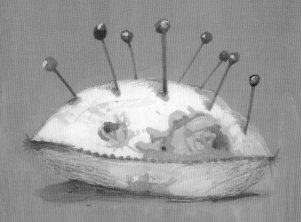

The Pantry

LA GIARDINIERA

LIMONCELLO

BASIL LIQUEUR

SALSA VERDE

TRUFFLE BUTTER

HERBED OILS & HERBED VINEGARS

ROSEMARY & SAGE SALT

ROSE SALT

VANILLA SALT

PEPPER SALT

STUFFED SMALL ROUND CHILES
WITH TUNA & ANCHOVY

RED RADICCHIO MARMALADE

NONNA'S PLUM & COGNAC MOSTARDA

CELERY MARMALADE

CHILE & RED PEPPER PRESERVES

ORANGE MARMALADE

PEACH PRESERVES

QUINCE JELLY & QUINCE PRESERVES

NONNA'S BLACKBERRIES AL NATURALE

PERFUMED SUGARS

What you sow you will reap and can then heap into jars.
Your work will be well rewarded through the colder months,
and the jars and bottles will add a good splash of color to the
paler days and darker winter nights. They will brighten your
pantry and pepper your meals. Giovanni often comes home
with boxes from Wilma, packaged in ways only she knows how.

SAPIENTE

WORDS/PAROLE

WORDS OF WISDOM

Mushrooms, tomatoes, onions, and sauces accommodated
into jars. Quinces shining like treasures from the bottom
and olive oils, glistening like newly dressed soldiers,
flanking the sides. And there's always a piece of cake or
savory cardoon pie that someone may have brought her, and
notes and other things tucked in…

LA GIARDINIERA

You won't believe how easy this is once you have the ingredients. You could even make a quarter of this amount.

I like to leave some of the vegetables whole or in large chunks so they look beautiful in the jars. You can use any vegetables you like; the more colors you have, the merrier. The shallots from Tropea in southern Italy are a beautiful red and come in all different sizes and they are lovely in this recipe. The larger ones will have to be halved or chunked to allow the vinegar to penetrate.

Using olive oil alone will make this too heavy, so I use one part olive oil to four parts sunflower oil.

2¾ POUNDS BELL PEPPERS,
HALF RED AND HALF
YELLOW, STEMS AND
SEEDS REMOVED, CUT INTO
NICE CHUNKY PIECES

2 SMALL EGGPLANTS, HALVED
OR QUARTERED LENGTHWISE,
THEN CUT INTO THICK SLICES

2 POUNDS SHALLOTS

1¼ POUNDS SMALL CARROTS,
SCRUBBED, WITH SOME
GREEN TOPS ATTACHED

7 OUNCES GREEN
BEANS, TRIMMED

14 OUNCES FIRM INNER
CELERY STALKS WITH
SOME LEAVES

1¾ POUNDS TRIMMED
CAULIFLOWER, CUT
INTO LARGE FLORETS

2 LONG FENNEL BULBS, CUT
LENGTHWISE INTO 6 WEDGES
ATTACHED AT THE BASE

8 CUPS COLD WATER

3⅓ CUPS COARSE SALT

8 CUPS WHITE WINE VINEGAR

SMALL FISTFUL OF
BLACK PEPPERCORNS

3 TO 4 SMALL CHILES,
DRIED OR FRESH

8 CUPS SUNFLOWER OIL

2 CUPS OLIVE OIL

Makes a lot

Put all the prepared vegetables in a large bucket or basin—wherever they will fit. Cover with the water, salt, and vinegar and leave overnight with a weight on so they are all immersed. The next day, drain away the liquid, letting the vegetables sit for a while in a colander. You can rinse the beans now if you think they will be too salty. Cover four large trays with kitchen towels. Lay the vegetables on the trays in a single layer. Cover with a food umbrella and leave them for a few hours or even overnight.

Have clean, sterilized jars (see page 330) ready—as large or small as are suitable for you. Pack the vegetables compactly into the jars along with some peppercorns and at least one chile in each jar. Cover with oil, starting with the sunflower oil and finishing with the olive oil. If the vegetables are not covered, just top up with more of either oil. Leave them awhile for the oils to settle, pressing out any air bubbles that may be trapped. You can put a plastic holder over the vegetables in each jar to make sure they are completely immersed in the oil. Cover with the lids and store in the pantry for at least 2 to 4 weeks before eating.

8 LEMONS

4 CUPS PURE ALCOHOL (MOST
ARE BETWEEN 96 AND 98%)

5 CUPS SUGAR

Makes about 10 cups

LIMONCELLO

*It's such a great feeling to produce this beautiful
liqueur, the color of dusty lemons, on your very own.
It is desirable to use unsprayed lemons from the
Amalfi Coast, but get what you can.*

*We don't need the lemons here, only the skins,
so I will direct you to the Lemon Pie (page 296). When
your limoncello is ready you can make Limoncello
Sorbet (page 322) or just drink it pure. This recipe is from
Massimo, Giovanni's friend, and he got it from his Sicilian
friend's grandmother. There you go. I love this exchanging
of recipes. It's a good idea to mark the date on the carafe
as you work, in case you don't remember how long the
lemon zest has been macerating.*

You will need a large, wide-mouthed glass carafe of 12
cups or so.

Wash the lemons very well and scrub the skins. Pare
them with a potato peeler or paring knife into good strips,
taking care to only get the yellow part, not the white pith.
Put them in the carafe, cover with the alcohol, and leave
to macerate for 1 week, covered. Give the carafe a shake
every so often to make sure all the zest is covered.

Put the sugar and 4 cups of water in a saucepan
and stir until the sugar has dissolved. Bring to a boil and
simmer for just under 10 minutes. Remove from the heat.
Using cheesecloth or a fine strainer, strain the alcohol into
a pitcher (we don't need the lemon zest any more). Slowly
pour the alcohol over the hot syrup in the pan, taking care
as it will spit out at you. Let cool completely. Pour back
into the carafe, cover again, and leave for 10 to 15 days.
It will now be ready to drink. You can pour it into smaller
clear glass bottles if you like, such as the bottle the alcohol
came in.

Serve well chilled (you can even keep it in the freezer).
It is lovely in summer.

BASIL LIQUEUR

4 CUPS PURE ALCOHOL (MOST
ARE BETWEEN 96 AND 98%)

80 BASIL LEAVES

ZEST OF 4 LEMONS,
YELLOW PART ONLY

3⅔ CUPS SUGAR

———

Makes about 10 cups

Marisa passed this recipe on to me and it was given to her by a contadina *who makes up many concoctions of her own. I love the way she uses a pot, even though it doesn't need any cooking. It's a great way to use up 80 leaves of basil when the plant is rolling out its leaves in abundance.*

Put the alcohol, basil, lemon zest, sugar, and 4 cups of water in a pot or wide-necked carafe and cover. Leave for 1 week to 10 days, stirring it each day with a wooden spoon or giving the carafe a shake. Strain with cheesecloth or a fine strainer into clear bottles. Use the bottle the alcohol came in if it's nice. It is ready to drink immediately. Serve it well chilled after a meal.

SALSA VERDE

2½ TABLESPOONS
CHOPPED PARSLEY

2½ TABLESPOONS
CHOPPED TARRAGON

1 HEAPING TABLESPOON
CHOPPED MINT

2 MEDIUM CLOVES GARLIC,
FINELY CHOPPED

2½ TABLESPOONS DRAINED
CAPERS IN VINEGAR (WITH
A LITTLE VINEGAR LEFT
CLINGING), CHOPPED

3 ANCHOVY FILLETS, CHOPPED

1 TEASPOON DIJON MUSTARD

⅔ CUP OLIVE OIL

PINCH OF CHILI POWDER

FRESHLY GROUND BLACK PEPPER

———

Makes about ¾ cup

This is a lovely sauce that is traditionally served with boiled meats, but it also works beautifully with broiled meats and vegetables. It will keep for a few days in the fridge but it must be covered with a layer of olive oil.

Put the herbs in a bowl and add the garlic, capers, and anchovies. Mix the mustard and olive oil together in a small bowl, then stir this into the herb mixture. Add the chili powder and a few good grinds of black pepper. Taste and adjust the seasoning as needed. Cover and put in the fridge for a while for the flavors to mingle.

SAPIENTE
WORDS/PAROLE

KEEP A FRESH WILD CHESTNUT
IN YOUR POCKET TO ENSURE YOU
DON'T CATCH A COLD.

¾ OUNCE WHITE TRUFFLE

2 TABLESPOONS
BUTTER, SOFTENED

1 TEASPOON
OLIVE OIL

SALT AND FRESHLY
GROUND BLACK PEPPER

———

Makes about ¼ cup

TRUFFLE BUTTER

*This is a luxurious butter for those wonderful times when
you can get fresh truffles. I use white truffle here but you
can also use black. The intensity of your truffle butter will
depend on the truffle season. This is a humble amount,
but if you were to make more the proportion of truffle
to butter would be less. For example, if you had
7 ounces of truffles, then you would probably need about
2¼ pounds of butter. Keep any butter you don't use
immediately in the freezer to preserve its strength.*

*You can keep your truffle (or truffles) buried in rice,
then use the rice with its lingering perfume to make
a risotto with butter and Parmesan.*

Clean the truffle (or truffles) well with a stiff brush, making
sure to get rid of any attached soil. Shave or slice very
finely, then chop. Mix into the butter with the olive oil,
a little salt if your butter is unsalted, and a few grinds of
black pepper. Keep in a closed jar in the fridge to use
soon, or pat into a log and wrap in waxed paper, then
plastic wrap, and freeze. Cut slices as needed.

HERBED OILS

THE
LIST

HERBED OILS WILL KEEP
FOR UP TO 6 MONTHS IF
IN STERILIZED BOTTLES
(SEE PAGE 330)

I love having a row of bottles of oils with herbs and things dropped into them. Apart from how they look, they add depth to a salad dressing or anything that might need a splash of oil.

You can top up the oil when necessary and add extra flavorings. Just make sure the flavorings are covered with the oil. You will need a bottle with a spouted cork on top for drizzling.

Things that flavor oils nicely are garlic, chiles, fresh herbs, spices such as pink, black, or green peppercorns, and even flowers like lavender and rose.

Choose an oil that is not too heavy or strong, as this could mask or clash with the flavorings added.

HERBED VINEGARS

HERBED VINEGARS WILL
KEEP FOR UP TO
6 MONTHS IF IN STERILIZED
BOTTLES (SEE PAGE 330)

Wilma says that years ago, when vinegar was a bit weak or the bottle was getting low, they'd put four or five strands of uncooked spaghetti in it. The starch of the pasta helped strengthen the vinegar. They would also add the leftovers from a bottle of wine, pouring it through a paper towel to hold back any fondo. This would then make more vinegar. But you had to have the mother, the starter, in there.

To help the fermentation, they would use a piece of paper for a cork. This would allow the vinegar to breathe.

Things that nicely flavor vinegar include lemon zest, chiles, garlic, herbs such as tarragon, and spices such as peppercorns, coriander seeds, and allspice.

Choose a base vinegar by strength, flavor, and color. For example, you could use cider vinegar, or white or red wine vinegar, or a combination of the two for a rosé blush.

Infuse the vinegar for a week or two before using. The vinegar will last as long as the flavorings are covered.

ROSEMARY & SAGE SALT

6 TABLESPOONS
CHOPPED ROSEMARY

6 TABLESPOONS
CHOPPED SAGE

2 MEDIUM CLOVES
GARLIC, CHOPPED

1 SMALL RED CHILE,
CHOPPED

½ CUP PINK HIMALAYAN SALT
(OR OTHER COARSE SALT)

A FEW BLACK PEPPERCORNS

———

Makes about 1¼ cups

This is great to always have in your kitchen, to scatter over meats and potatoes before roasting. The herbs will perfume and flavor the salt beautifully. It's up to you as to how much you use, and you can be less heavy-handed if you prefer less salt. You will need a good amount of lovely fresh rosemary and sage. Strip the leaves off their branches before chopping them.

Scatter the rosemary, sage, garlic, and chile on a tray lined with waxed paper. Cover with a food umbrella and put in front of a window that gets direct sunlight.

Crush the salt in small batches in a mortar with a pestle. It's nice to have varying texture in the salt, but each crystal should be at least cracked. Crush the peppercorns with the last batch. Toss onto the tray with the herbs and leave to dry, then store in a closed jar.

ROSE SALT

½ CUP PINK HIMALAYAN
SALT (OR OTHER
COARSE SALT)

ABOUT 3 TABLESPOONS
TINY, DRIED, EXQUISITELY
PERFUMED UNSPRAYED
DAMASCUS ROSES,
OR OTHER EDIBLE
ROSES OR PETALS

———

Makes about ¾ cup

Rose salt adds a lovely scented layer to a dish. I love having this kind of accessory sitting on my countertop for its persistent lingering perfume.

In a mortar, crush the salt in batches with a pestle until it looks like crushed diamonds. Some crystals will be fine and others still coarse, but each diamond should have been at least gently cracked so you don't have rocks on your plate. A little bite is lovely though.

Pour the salt into a bowl. Put the roses in the mortar and crush gently with the pestle to release many of the petals, but don't pulverize them. Stop when they look gorgeous and shake them out into your salt. Remove any dark inner bits that don't look great. Stir gently. Breathe.

Keeps for many months in a tightly closed container or box. Stir gently before using.

VANILLA SALT

THE
LIST

½ CUP PINK HIMALAYAN SALT
(OR OTHER COARSE SALT)

2 PLUMP VANILLA BEANS

2 TEASPOONS VANILLA
EXTRACT

———

Makes about ¹/₂ cup

I love to sprinkle this over fish or salads and vegetables. These amounts are just approximate. You may make as much or as little as you like. You can also tuck in a rinsed and dried vanilla bean that you have used elsewhere.

Preheat the oven to 350°F.

In a mortar, pound the salt in batches with a pestle. Some salt will be fine and some will be coarse, which is perfect. Pour into a bowl. Split the vanilla beans down their length with a small sharp knife and halve. Scrape out the seeds with the tip of the knife into the salt, then scatter the vanilla extract over. Take some salt in your hands and massage the beans to get as many vanilla seeds as possible into the salt and mix the vanilla extract through. Add the vanilla bean pods.

Pour the salt onto a baking sheet lined with waxed paper and bake for 5 to 6 minutes, to dry it out. Remove from the oven and let cool, then set aside until completely dry. Pour into a container or box that you can close tightly and leave for a week or two before using, stirring every now and then so it is well distributed. Keeps for a long time.

PEPPER SALT

½ CUP PINK HIMALAYAN SALT
(OR OTHER COARSE SALT)

2 TEASPOONS BLACK
PEPPERCORNS

2 TEASPOONS PINK
PEPPERCORNS

———

Makes about ¹/₂ cup

This is nice, easy and very convenient to have ready. I use it in the Salt & Pepper Potatoes with a Trickle of Buttermilk (page 110) and it is also lovely scattered over broiled steaks, chicken, or fish.

Crush the salt in a mortar with a pestle, a bit at a time. Pour into a bowl. Crush half the peppercorns with just one crack and the rest a little more. Mix together with the salt. Store in a closed box. Give it a gentle shake before using.

STUFFED SMALL ROUND CHILES WITH TUNA & ANCHOVY

ABOUT 50 SMALL
ROUND RED CHILES

2 CUPS WHITE VINEGAR

10 BLACK PEPPERCORNS

5 WHOLE CLOVES

1 (14-OUNCE) CAN TUNA
IN OIL, WELL DRAINED

3½ OUNCES ANCHOVY
FILLETS, WELL DRAINED

5½ OUNCES CAPERS IN
VINEGAR, WELL DRAINED

OLIVE OIL, TO COVER THE
CHILES IN THE JARS

Makes several jars

You will need wide-necked sterilized jars (see page 330) to accommodate these beauties. I hope you can find gorgeous round jewels of chiles, such as these. Small ones are a lovely monodose that you can just pop in your mouth, while bigger ones can be shared.

Use thin gloves when working with the chiles so your hands don't burn for the rest of the day.

The amount of filling you'll need will vary, depending on the size of your chiles. Mine were all different, which looks lovely in the jar. Just make up extra filling if needed, and if you have too much serve the leftovers on crostini.

Cover a couple of baking sheets with clean kitchen towels. Rinse the chiles. Put the vinegar in a not-too-wide pot—you will need enough to just cover the chiles. Bring to a boil, then add the peppercorns and cloves, and dive in the chiles in batches so they all get a full chance in the vinegar. Let it come back to a boil and then boil for 3 or 4 minutes, but no more. Transfer to the lined sheets with a slotted spoon (return any peppercorns or cloves to the vinegar), then add the next batch to the vinegar and so on, until they are all done. Leave to cool.

Use a small, sharp knife to cut out the hat of each chile without piercing or removing any flesh. As you pull the hat away many of the seeds will come with it, but you will need a very small teaspoon to remove the rest of the seeds, taking special care not to break the chiles. Best to sit down and relax while you do this, with a trash bin in front of you and thin gloves on your hands. Arrange the chiles back on the sheet for now. You can discard the seeds or you might like to plant them.

Put the tuna, anchovies, and capers on a board and chop them well, but not completely smoothly; some texture is good. You can pulse them in a food processor if you like. Mix them together to make a well-blended paste.

Now, fill the chiles. Holding a chile in one hand (again wearing gloves), grab some of the paste and stuff it into the belly of the chile, pressing down well with your fingers so it is tight and firmly packed, nearly flush. Carefully put the stuffed chiles in the jars, sitting them upright and nestled close to one another. Gently pour olive oil over them, then wait for the level to settle and add more as necessary to completely cover the chiles. You can put a plastic holder on top to keep the chiles submerged.

The chiles will need a few weeks in the jar before serving for the flavors to mix well. The jars can be kept on a shelf in the pantry until opened, then put them in the fridge. The oil will congeal but it needs just a short while at room temperature to return to its glossy old self.

RED RADICCHIO MARMALADE

This is great with mature pecorino or other cheeses. It also works well with boiled meats and is particularly nice with game. Lovely with sausages, too.

Quarter the radicchio and remove the thick white stems. Shred the leaves, not too coarsely. Heat the oil in a wide, heavy-bottomed pot and sauté the radicchio until it has surrendered a bit. Add the sugar, wine, vinegar, lemon juice, raisins, bay leaf, chili powder, apples, and 1 cup of water, some salt, and a few grinds of black pepper. Simmer, partly covered, for about 1½ hours, until it has reduced and is thick and a bit jammy looking. Remove the lid and simmer for another 30 minutes or until most of the liquid has gone, stirring often. Ladle into warm sterilized jars (see page 330), seal with the lids, and turn upside down.

Leave to cool before turning upright, creating a vacuum. Store in the pantry until opened, then keep in the fridge.

THE
LIST

2¼ POUNDS ROUND
RED RADICCHIO

5 TABLESPOONS OLIVE OIL

3 CUPS SUGAR

1 CUP RED WINE

3 TABLESPOONS
BALSAMIC VINEGAR

3 TABLESPOONS FRESHLY
SQUEEZED LEMON JUICE

⅓ CUP ZIBBIBO RAISINS (SEE
GLOSSARY, PAGE 329) OR
SMALL SEEDLESS MUSCATELS

1 BAY LEAF

A GOOD FEW PINCHES
OF CHILI POWDER

2 APPLES, CORED AND
COARSELY SHREDDED

SALT AND FRESHLY
GROUND BLACK PEPPER

Makes about 4 cups

NONNA'S PLUM & COGNAC MOSTARDA

THE LIST

2¼ POUNDS PLUMS

3½ CUPS SUGAR

1 CINNAMON STICK

2½ TABLESPOONS
MUSTARD POWDER

½ CUP COGNAC

Makes 4 cups

This is good to make when plums are at their best, so you can enjoy their flavor for the rest of the year. It is lovely next to roasted meats or even cold meats and cheeses.

Halve the plums and discard the stones. Put the plum halves in a large bowl, scatter the sugar on top, and leave for 12 hours, covered with a kitchen towel.

Scrape everything into a nonreactive metal pot and bring slowly to a boil, stirring often. Boil, uncovered, for 10 minutes. Remove from the heat and allow to cool, then cover. After 12 hours, add the cinnamon stick and then boil again, uncovered, for 10 minutes. Remove from the heat, allow to cool, and leave, covered, for another 12 hours.

Mix the mustard and cognac together in a small bowl, then stir this into the plums. Bring to a boil and simmer, uncovered, for about 15 minutes, or until a teaspoonful dropped onto a plate clings, rather than runs, when the plate is tilted. Overcooking will make the *mostarda* too firm. Bottle while hot into warm sterilized jars (see page 330). Seal with the lids and turn upside down. Leave to cool before turning upright, creating a vacuum. Store in the pantry until opened, then keep in the fridge.

CELERY
MARMALADE

THE
LIST

1 BUNCH CELERY (ABOUT
3¾ POUNDS)

5 CUPS SUGAR

GOOD PINCH OF CHILI FLAKES

FINELY GRATED ZEST OF
1 LEMON, YELLOW PART ONLY

JUICE OF 1 LEMON

⅔ CUP WHITE WINE

4 TABLESPOONS GRAPPA

Makes 4 cups

This is beautiful with a mixed cheese plate and alongside ham. The grappa is there to keep the good green color, says Wilma. It's a good idea to fill various small jars so they don't stay open for too long in the fridge.

Wash and trim the celery, and cut into stalks. You will need about 10 ounces of inner ones with their leaves and $1^1/_3$ pounds of thick outer ones. Leave the inner ones to one side for now. String the thick stalks with a small, sharp paring knife by digging in at one end of the stalk, then lifting the strings and dragging them down. Strip all the strings away or they will just end up in your marmalade. Chop up roughly, then blitz in a food processor, but don't make it too fine as some small bits are good.

The tender inner stalks probably won't need stripping. Slice these and their leaves into rounds so they will show up in your jars. Put all the celery in a suitable pot with the sugar, chili flakes, lemon zest and juice, wine, and ⅔ cup of water, and bring to a gentle boil. Lower the heat and simmer, uncovered, stirring extremely often to check that nothing is sticking or caramelizing. If it seems to be going along too quickly and the sugar is getting ahead of the celery, add a little more water. Continue simmering and stirring for 45 minutes to an hour, until it is a bit jammy but still loose.

To test when it is ready, drop a teaspoonful onto a small saucer and tilt. It shouldn't slide down easily, but drag with a little resistance. Add the grappa and let it cook for a couple of minutes more, then turn off the heat. Ladle into warm sterilized jars (see page 330). Seal the lids tightly and turn the jars upside down. Leave to cool before turning upright, creating a vacuum. Store in the pantry until opened, then keep in the fridge.

2¼ POUNDS BRIGHT
RED PEPPERS

8½ OUNCES SMALL
RED CHILES

5 CUPS SUGAR

2 TABLESPOONS RED
WINE VINEGAR

Makes about 5 cups

CHILE & RED PEPPER PRESERVES

This is sweet and hot, a beautiful thing to whip out and serve next to almost anything. Its strength will depend on the type of chiles you use. Choose ones that are soft, a beautiful red, and not drying out. I like to use jars of varying sizes. Be sure to label them so you remember what's inside.

Remove the stems and seeds from the peppers. Roughly cut up the flesh directly into a large, heavy-bottomed pot. Wearing gloves, remove the tops from the chiles, then slice them lengthwise and scrape out the seeds. You will need about 5½ ounces of cleaned chiles, depending on their strength. Take extreme care when working with chiles that the seeds are not flying all over the kitchen and remember not to touch your skin or eyes, as it can burn for ages. Rinse, then cut them up roughly and put in the pot. It's okay if a few seeds go in.

Add the sugar, vinegar, and ½ cup of water and bring to a boil, then slightly lower the heat to a steady simmer. Partly cover and simmer for about an hour to soften the chiles. Pulse until smooth with a handheld blender directly in the pot. Return to the heat and simmer, uncovered, for 15 minutes or longer if necessary to thicken up slightly. To test when the preserves are ready, drop a teaspoonful onto a small saucer and tilt. It should not slip down easily, but slide with a little resistance.

Have warm sterilised jars (see page 330) ready for filling. Funnel in the preserves, or ladle it into a pitcher and then pour into the jars, taking care not to burn yourself. Put the lids on, close tightly, and then turn the jars upside down. Leave to cool before turning upright, creating a vacuum. Store in the pantry until opened, then keep in the fridge.

SAPIENTE
WORDS/PAROLE

ORANGE
MARMALADE

◇◇

THE
LIST

4½ POUNDS ORANGES

1 LEMON

5⅓ CUPS SUGAR

4 TABLESPOONS COGNAC

Makes about 6 cups

Try to get seedless oranges to save you the step of removing the seeds. Use unsprayed oranges and scrub the skins well beforehand.

Prick the oranges all over with a toothpick, put in a large nonreactive pot, and cover with warm water. Cut the zest off the lemon in thin strips and add to the oranges, along with the juice of the lemon. Leave for 12 hours.

Drain the oranges and cut away their top hats. Cut them into thin slices, then cut those into quarters. Put in a large, heavy-bottomed pot, add the sugar, and leave to macerate, covered, for 12 hours. Now put the pot over a low flame and bring to a boil. Simmer, uncovered, for 1½ hours, then add 3 cups of hot water. Simmer for another 1½ hours, adding another 3 cups or so of hot water during this time as the marmalade reduces. The zest should be translucent and tender, and there should be a nice amount of thickened liquid.

To test when it is ready, drop a teaspoonful onto a small saucer and tilt. It should not slip down easily, but slide with a little resistance. Add the cognac and simmer for a few minutes more before removing from the heat. Distribute among warm sterilized jars (see page 330), seal with the lids and turn upside down. Leave to cool before turning upright, creating a vacuum. Store in the pantry until opened, then keep in the fridge.

PEACH PRESERVES

THE LIST

2¼ POUNDS RIPE PEACHES

2½ CUPS SUGAR

2½ TABLESPOONS AMARETTO

———

Makes about 4 cups

Many ladies I have questioned say that peach preserves are their favorite. This is a lovely recipe, with just three ingredients. It is quite a loose preserve and I like it that way. Serve it with bread for breakfast or use it to fill a crostata.

The peaches must be sweet and ripe. Keep a few of the peach pits to add to your preserve while it cooks, as these give another layer of flavor.

Halve the peaches, leaving the skins on. Remove the pits, keeping about four aside. Put the peaches in a pot suitable for making preserves and cover with 1 cup of water. Put the lid on and simmer for about 20 minutes to soften the peaches. Pulse with a handheld blender directly in the pot until smooth. Now add the sugar and the saved pits. Bring back to a boil, then lower the heat and simmer for about 1 hour, stirring with a wooden spoon very regularly to check that nothing is sticking. Do the plate test; drop a teaspoonful onto a small saucer and tilt. It should not slip down easily, but cling.

When the preserve is ready add the amaretto and cook for a couple of minutes more. Ladle into warm sterilized jars (see page 330), seal with the lids, and turn upside down. Leave to cool before turning upright, creating a vacuum. Store in the pantry until opened, then keep in the fridge.

SAPIENTE

WORDS/PAROLE

QUINCES CAN BE KEPT IN THE LINEN
CUPBOARD FOR THE LOVELY FRAGRANCE
THEY GIVE (IN A BOWL SO THEY
DON'T STAIN ANYTHING).

QUINCE JELLY

THE LIST

4½ RIPE QUINCES

1 LEMON

2½ CUPS SUGAR

———

Makes 3 cups

The quinces in this recipe can be cooked in a pressure cooker, which would reduce the cooking time by around a third and maintain a good water level, too. Wilma doesn't let anything go to waste and uses the cooked pulp to make Quince Preserves (see opposite).

Cut the quinces into small chunks, cores and all, and the lemon into quarters. Put them all in a deep nonreactive pot and cover with plenty of water. Bring to a boil and simmer gently, partly covered, until the fruit is soft and the liquid is a lovely fuchsia pink. This can take anywhere from 2 hours on, so check often by piercing the fruit with a small, sharp knife. Resist the temptation to add extra water during cooking.

Wet and wring out a jelly bag or line a large colander with damp cheesecloth and sit it over a bowl. Pour in the fruit and leave, without stirring or pressing, until all the juice has run through. Overnight is good.

Measure the juice, then pour it into a large enameled or stainless-steel pan. Save the quince pulp to make preserves, but discard the lemon quarters. Weigh out 1¼ pounds of sugar for every 4 cups of juice and add to the pan. Stir over medium heat until the sugar has dissolved, then bring to a boil. Skim any scum from the surface.

Simmer, uncovered, until the setting point is reached, about 45 minutes. To check if it's ready, dab a little between your fingers and pull them slowly apart—the jelly should form a slightly sticky string. Pour into warm sterilized jars (see page 330). Seal well, turn upside down, and leave to cool. Turn the jars upright, creating a vacuum. Store in the pantry until opened, then keep in the fridge.

QUINCE PRESERVES

Remove the cores and seeds from the quince pulp. Put the quinces through a ricer or mash with a potato masher. Weigh the puree and allow 17 ounces sugar for every 2 pounds of puree. Put the sugar, puree, wine, and lemon zest and juice in a nonreactive, heavy-bottomed pan. Bring to a boil, then simmer slowly for 30 minutes, stirring almost continuously, until you have a lovely thick preserve. It is important that it is on low heat and that you stir regularly so that it doesn't burn.

Do the plate test: drop a teaspoonful onto a saucer and tilt. The preserves should cling rather than slip down easily, and should wrinkle when poked. Pour into warm sterilized jars (see page 330). Seal with the lids and turn upside down. Leave to cool before turning upright, creating a vacuum. Store in the pantry until opened, then keep in the fridge.

NONNA'S BLACKBERRIES AL NATURALE

This is a great way to keep blackberries going a little longer, or any fruits, really—cherries, grapes, plums in pieces, and so on. I like them like this, not too sweet, though you can use more sugar if you like. They are wonderful al naturale or served with a scoop of Fior di Latte Ice Cream (page 323).

Put the blackberries in two 3-cup jars. The volume collapses a lot during cooking so don't press down and squash them. Scatter 2½ tablespoons of sugar into each jar, then seal. Bring a large pot of water to a boil. Wrap the jars in cloths, secured with string, to avoid them clunking around. Keep the ends of the string long and use them to lower the jars into the water—the water must cover them, so add more boiling water if necessary. Cover with a heavy plate to keep the jars submerged and boil for about 15 minutes. Turn off the heat and leave the jars in the water to cool completely, creating a vacuum. Store in the pantry until opened, then keep in the fridge, but not for too long.

PERFUMED SUGARS

Scented sugars are a wonderful addition to any kitchen and are simple to make. Here are a few examples. They can be used in creams, cookies, cakes, or just scattered over fruit salads.

LAVENDER SUGAR

⅔ CUP SUGAR

1 TEASPOON UNSPRAYED
LAVENDER FLOWERS

Beautiful for making cookies or whipping into a cream.

Put the sugar and lavender in a box and shake gently, like you're shaking maracas. Leave for a couple of weeks, shaking the box every now and then. When you are getting really good at the shaking, the lavender should have perfumed the sugar. You can use the sugar with the lavender in it, or sift it out if you prefer.

ROSE SUGAR

⅔ CUP SUGAR

1 HANDFUL OF DRIED, FRAGRANT
UNSPRAYED ROSE PETALS

Use petals with a beautiful scent, which you have dried well.

Put the sugar over the petals in a bowl and stir. Cover with a food umbrella or similar to allow air to flow through. Leave for a week or so for the petals to perfume the sugar before using.

LEMON VERBENA SUGAR

⅔ CUP SUGAR

18 LEMON VERBENA LEAVES

Pick the beautifully fragrant verbena leaves, spread them over a tray, and leave to dry for a few days.

Put the sugar and dried leaves in a lovely tin and shake. Leave for a couple of weeks to perfume, shaking the tin every now and then. You can leave the verbena in the sugar until you use it.

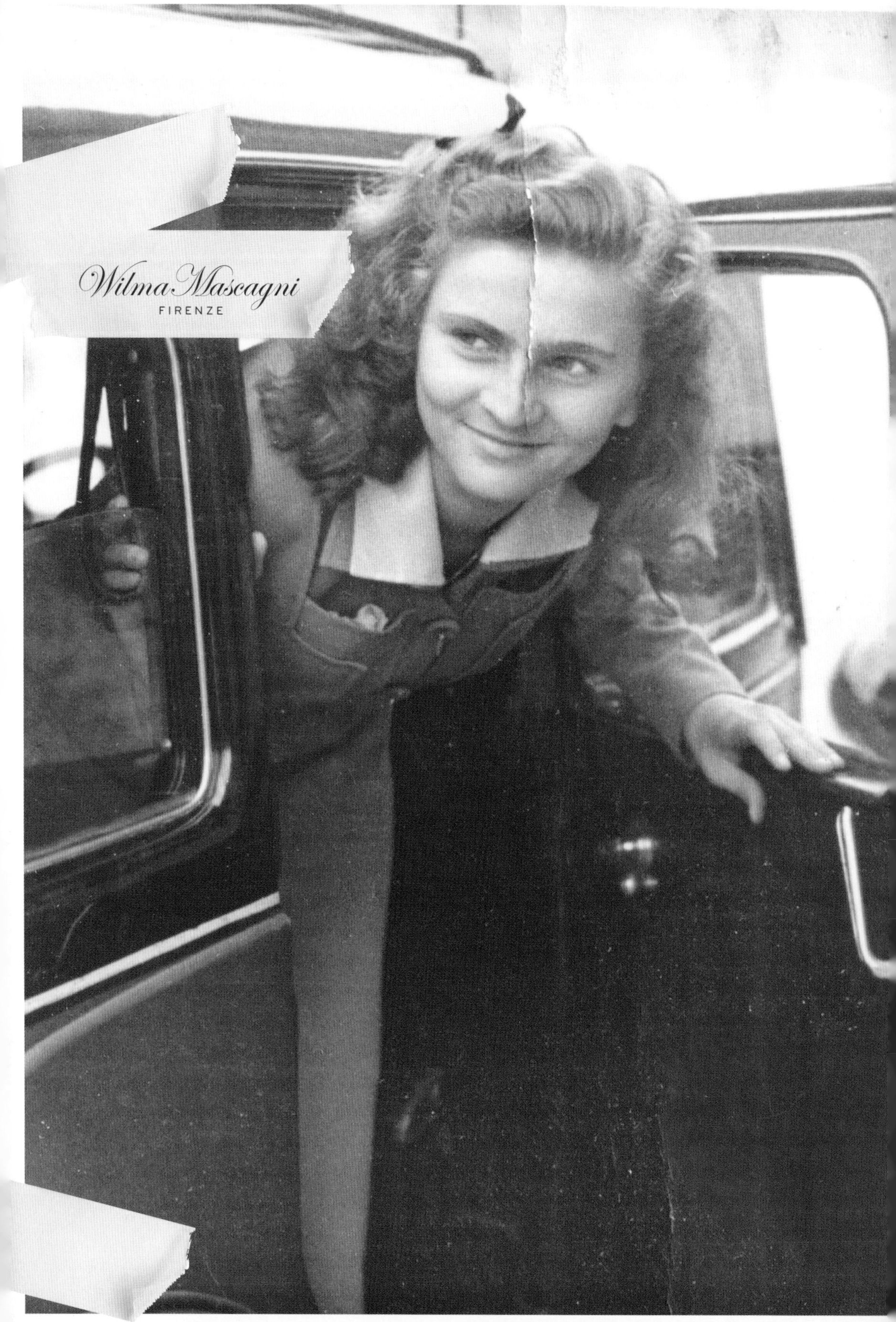
Wilma Mascagni
FIRENZE

3

The Bread Oven

✳

CIABATTA (SOUL DOUGH)

Giovanni said "soul dough" instead of sourdough once—it's a perfect description. Ciabatta is my soul dough.

There are longer routes to ciabatta. This is quite quick. I love this bread for its irregular shape, the flour that stays on the lovely crust, and its spacious interior. It is great cut into panini and stuffed with various fillings, such as the Baked Crumbed Chicken (page 171).

For the starter, crumble or place the yeast into the water in a deep, sturdy bowl. Add the flour and sugar and mix together with a wooden spoon to a nice sloppy dough (it will be too sticky to use your hands). Cover with plastic wrap, then a kitchen towel, and leave in a warm draft-free spot for an hour or longer, until it has puffed and is bubbly.

Add the rest of the ingredients, and add ¾ cup of water, and mix in initially with the wooden spoon. The dough will be very sticky, but resist the temptation to add more flour. When everything is combined, use floured hands to pull and slap it around in the bowl until springy, 1 to 2 minutes. It will be too sticky to knead. Cover and leave again until full of air and puffy, a good 2 hours or more.

Line a baking sheet with waxed paper and scatter a good handful of flour over it. Scatter flour over a big wooden board and make a little pile to the side. Press your hands in this to cover them with flour, then divide the dough in half. Just use the flour that is on the board and what you bring over on your hands. Stretch and pat each half into a long, flat loaf, about 12 inches long and 6 inches wide more or less; you want it to be lovely and irregular. Carefully put the breads on the prepared sheet, allowing for expansion, and scatter a little extra flour on top. Cover with a food umbrella (or a similar structure that will allow for the bread's expansion without touching it) and then a kitchen towel. Leave in a warm spot for 1 to 1½ hours, until nice and puffy.

Preheat the oven to 415°F. Bake the loaves until crusty and lightly golden, about 25 minutes. Remove from the oven and transfer to a wire rack so the crust stays crisp as the bread cools. Each ciabatta can be cut into four for panini, if you like.

POLISH PUFF PASTRY

This isn't as hard to make as its reputation holds. You can drink a cup of herbal tea in between each chilling time and get on with whatever you are doing. The result is soft, wonderful, layered, buttery, and well worth it. Incidentally, this recipe comes from Olga, the Ukrainian-Polish housekeeper who was looking after Marzia's elderly mom. In addition to her pastry making, Olga is known for having hands of gold—wonderful at working lace, darning, and mending small details no one else can do.

Pile the flour in a heap in a wide bowl and add the salt. Put the butter around the outside of the flour, tossing it very lightly in the outskirts to lightly coat. Make a well in the center of the flour and carefully pour in the water, working it in with one hand as you pour but without incorporating any butter. Keep mixing with your hand in a stirring motion until you have a soft dough. Now use both hands to work in the butter. If it seems to be melting before it is incorporated, use a large fork to work it in. Knead until you have a soft, smoothish dough—it doesn't matter if a few small unmelded bits of butter remain. Shape it into a flat block, wrap in plastic wrap, and put in the fridge for 20 minutes or so.

On a lightly floured board, roll the dough out to a long rectangle of about 9½ by 4 inches. Fold one end up two-thirds of the way, then the other end down to cover it, forming a *portafoglio* (purse). Put back in the fridge, covered with plastic wrap, for 20 minutes or until it is firm. Have a rest, a cup of herbal tea. Put the dough on the board, pointing in the same direction as before, then give it a half turn so that the folded ends are now at the sides. Roll out as before. Continue like this for a total of six times, each time chilling it for 20 minutes or so, covered with plastic wrap. Rest some more. Have another cup of herbal tea. As you progress, the dough will become smoother and easier to roll. You might find that some butter remains unincorporated, but don't worry—the main thing is to end up with a neat block of pastry with uniformly multiple layers.

Use immediately or keep in the fridge, covered, for 24 hours. Otherwise, store in the freezer, then defrost in the fridge. I use this for the Chicken Breast Pie (page 173) and the Ham & Green Olive Tart (page 65), and it can also be used for desserts.

FAST FOCACCIA WITH STRAWBERRIES

This is truly lovely. The kind of thing you like just being at the same table with. The strawberries must be incredible— sweet and bursting with flavor. If yours are not, you may need more sugar. You can serve this as a snack or for breakfast, it's something between a sweet and a bread.

Crumble or place the yeast into a large bowl and stir in the water with 1 heaping tablespoon of the sugar. Add the flour and salt and knead lightly, dipping your hands in a little flour if necessary, to give a soft, stickier than usual dough.

Flick a little water over a good-sized baking sheet 13 by 12 inches. Line with a piece of waxed paper, ironing the paper down with your hands so it sticks. Drizzle the olive oil on and spread this over the paper (with your hands if you like, for your skin to benefit from the great properties of olive oil). Now put the dough on the sheet and begin to spread it to completely cover the pan. It probably won't cooperate immediately, so stretch it to perhaps halfway, then leave it for 5 minutes or so and go back to it after its rest. Stretch and press it with your palms to edge it out to the sides of the pan. Cover with a food umbrella (or a similar structure that will allow for the dough's expansion). Leave it in a warm draft-free place to rise, about 1 to 1½ hours.

Meanwhile, rinse the strawberries and remove their green tops. Leave small ones whole, halve medium-size ones, and cut large ones into thirds. Put them in a bowl and scatter with 2½ heaping tablespoons of sugar. Stir them gently and leave at room temperature, covered.

Preheat the oven to 400°F. When the dough has puffed up nicely, gently stir the strawberries again, being careful not to break or mash them. Quickly and gently, so the dough doesn't deflate, place them all over the dough, keeping most of them upright so they look good once baked. Drizzle the juices here and there as you go. Scatter the remaining 1½ heaping tablespoons of sugar evenly over the top, right to the sides. Bake for about 25 minutes, or until the focaccia is golden and crisp on the edges and the strawberries have a lovely juicy look about them, almost scorched on a few edges. Make sure the middle part is cooked, too, turning the sheet around if necessary for the last 5 minutes. Don't overcook or the strawberries will collapse into a jam. Remove from the oven. Let cool. Shake confectioners' sugar over the top. Cut off pieces with kitchen scissors. Eat.

SAPIENTE

WORDS/PAROLE

FIRST DESERVE,
THEN DESIRE

EMILY'S BREAD

I just love the idea of this simple bread. I can picture Emily, picking up the breakfast things after everyone has vanished and then tipping all the leftovers into her baking bowl. How wonderfully wild. But yes, why throw these things out when you can produce a couple of loaves for the next meal?

Crumble or place the yeast into a large deep bowl and whisk in the water and sugar. When the yeast begins to bubble add the yogurt, olive oil, and coffee and mix with a wooden spoon to combine. Mix in the flour and then the salt to form a rather soft dough. Add a little more water or flour as necessary. Knead lightly for a few minutes in the bowl. Cover with a kitchen towel and leave in a warm, draft-free place until well puffed up, about 1½ hours.

Line a large baking sheet with waxed paper. Punch the dough down and divide into two portions. Shape into rather elongated loaves and make three diagonal slashes across each one. Put them on the lined sheet, leaving a good space in between. Cover again and leave in the warm spot until puffed and risen, about 1 hour.

Preheat the oven to 400°F. Bake the loaves for 20 to 25 minutes, until golden and crusty both underneath and on top. Transfer to a wire rack to cool.

This bread still tastes very good the next day and is also great toasted.

PIZZA MARGHERITA

There is something incredibly refreshing about a pizza margherita. You can't go wrong if your ingredients are beautiful. Its lovely name comes from Queen Margherita— it is said that when she was visiting Napoli the pizzaiolo made this pizza in her honor. You can use buffalo mozzarella in place of the regular mozzarella if you like. There will be enough dough for 4 pizzas, but I have only made 2 pizzas and used the rest for La Pizza Fritta (see opposite). If you need to keep any unused dough, wrap it in plastic wrap and store in the fridge overnight, or in the freezer.

Crumble or place the yeast into a small bowl and add the water and sugar. Put the flour in a large mixing bowl and make a well in the center. When the yeast starts to bubble, pour it into the flour. Mix with your hands to get a smooth soft dough, adding a little more water or flour as necessary. Mix in the salt, then knead the dough until very smooth and elastic, at least 5 minutes. Divide the dough equally between 2 bowls (you will have roughly 14 ounces in each bowl), cover each with a kitchen towel, and leave in a warm place to rise for about an hour, or until well puffed.

Meanwhile, place the tomatoes in a bowl (I like some chunks here), add 2½ tablespoons of the olive oil, and season with salt and black pepper. Tear 2 basil leaves in, mix well, and leave aside at room temperature, covered for now. Cut the mozzarella into slices and then into small blocks, leaving it on a tilted plate at room temperature so much of its liquid drains off.

Take one of the bowls, punch down the dough, and divide it into two balls. Cover them with a kitchen towel so they don't dry out (*pizzaioli* keep them in a drawer) and leave to rise again for about 20 minutes. Preheat the oven to 425°F.

Very lightly oil two 12½-inch-diameter pizza pans. Put a ball of dough on each tray. Using your palms and fingertips, press each ball of dough from the middle outward, to extend it to the edges of the pan. Sometimes this is easier if you take it halfway, let it rest for 5 minutes or so, and then finish taking it to the edge—it will move better after its rest. Dollop 1 cup of tomato onto the center of each pizza (the leftover tomato is for La Pizza Fritta).

Using the back of the ladle as the *pizzaioli* do, spread the sauce from the middle outward. Drizzle a generous tablespoon of olive oil over the top and put the pans in the oven.

Bake until the edges are golden in places and the underneath of the pizza is firm, not flabby and pale, about 15 minutes. Depending on your oven, it may be necessary to swap the sheets around halfway through. If you prefer, you can roll out and bake the pizzas one at a time. Take out the pizzas, scatter the mozzarella over them, and put back in the oven until the mozzarella melts, about 5 minutes. Serve hot, with a couple of fresh basil leaves scattered on top.

LA PIZZA FRITTA

THE
LIST

½ BATCH (14 OUNCES)
RISEN PIZZA DOUGH
(PRECEDING RECIPE)

LIGHT OLIVE OIL,
FOR PANFRYING

THE REMAINING TOMATO FROM
THE PRECEDING RECIPE, ABOUT
¾ CUP AT ROOM TEMPERATURE

7 OUNCES FRESH MOZZARELLA,
AT ROOM TEMPERATURE,
IN ½-INCH SLICES

A FEW BASIL LEAVES

Makes 4

Maybe we all look as good panfrying pizzas as Sophia Loren in the movie L'Oro di Napoli (The Gold of Naples)?

The cheese here doesn't get cooked so it is worth trying buffalo mozzarella or burrata, a very creamy fresh mozzarella, if you can get it. Otherwise, use a good-quality fresh mozzarella. These pizzas are surprisingly light.

Divide the dough into four equal balls. On a lightly floured board, pat each one out to a rough oval shape of about 8 by 6 inches. Pour enough oil into a wide skillet to cover the bottom.

Heat the oil and add the pizzas two at a time if they fit but if not, one by one. Panfry until golden underneath, then turn and panfry the other side until golden but not too dark. Remove with tongs and put on a plate lined with paper towels to drain. Immediately dollop some tomato on top, leaving the border free as one does with pizza, and top at once with mozzarella slices so they soften from the heat. Scatter a couple of basil leaves on top and serve hot.

SAPIENTE

WORDS/PAROLE

LONG AGO, WHEN THERE WERE
NO SUCH THINGS AS TIMERS,
IF SOMEONE ASKED HOW LONG
SOMETHING WOULD NEED IN
THE OVEN, THE ANSWER MAY
HAVE BEEN 'AS LONG AS IT
TAKES TO RECITE THREE
"AVE MARIAS"—AND THEN IT
WOULD BE ABOUT READY.

SWEET PIZZA

I've seen many Italians enjoying a sweet pizza after a savory one, even if it's just a slice. They make a lovely sweet finish to a meal and are great for sharing.

Preheat the oven to 400°F. Very lightly oil two 12½-inch diameter pizza pans. Divide the dough in half and put each portion on a pan. Using your palms and fingertips, press each portion of dough from the middle outward to extend it to the edges of the pan. Sometimes this is easier if you take it halfway, let it rest for 5 minutes or so and then finish taking it to the edge—it will move better after its rest.

Scatter the raspberries over one base and sprinkle with the sugar. The other base stays plain for now. Put both pans in the oven and bake for 10 to 12 minutes or until golden, swapping the pans around halfway through.

Meanwhile, toast the hazelnuts with a light sprinkling of salt in a dry skillet. Remove the pans from the oven. Dollop the chocolate spread over the plain base and spread gently with the back of the spoon, not quite all the way to the edge. Scatter the hazelnuts on top. Dust the raspberry pizza with confectioners' sugar and serve both warm.

DONZELLE

½ BATCH RISEN PIZZA DOUGH
(PAGE 56), ABOUT 14 OUNCES

LIGHT OLIVE OIL, FOR PANFRYING

6 TO 8 THIN SLICES OF
PROSCIUTTO, WITHOUT
TOO MUCH FAT

ABOUT 5½ OUNCES
STRACCHINO CHEESE (SEE
GLOSSARY, PAGE 329), AT
ROOM TEMPERATURE

Makes 12 to 14

Everyone seems to love these fried puffs, which are often made spontaneously from excess pizza or bread dough. They must be served hot and plain with a light sprinkling of salt. They make a fine meal or a starter, served in a basket with a plate of sliced prosciutto and another of stracchino to fill them. Stracchino is a soft, fresh, rindless, cow's milk cheese that has a mild taste.
You need to have a generous amount of oil in the pan for the donzelle *to cook properly. Sometimes they are served with a good shaking of confectioners' sugar instead of salt.*

Tear donzelle off pieces of dough and roll out or shape them into rough squares of 1½ by 2 inches, or roll to make cigars. Leave to rise, covered (the timing is not important). You can shape or roll and panfry as you go, so you have some dough rising while you're preparing and panfrying others.

Heat enough oil in a wide pan to cover the base. Gently drop the puffs in the hot oil in batches and panfry until golden on both sides. Remove with tongs to a tray lined with paper towels. Scatter a few grains of salt over each and serve immediately with the prosciutto and stracchino. Eat them split and filled like a panino or with the fillings draped on top, or serve them simply sprinkled with salt.

SAPIENTE
WORDS/PAROLE

**BLOSSOM WHERE
YOU ARE PLANTED.**

HAM & GREEN
OLIVE TART

THE
LIST

9 OUNCES POLISH PUFF
PASTRY (PAGE 51)

3 EGGS

1 CUP HEAVY CREAM

1¾ OUNCES FRESHLY
SHREDDED PARMESAN

5½ OUNCES THINLY SLICED
HAM, ROUGHLY CHOPPED

4¼ OUNCES PITTED GREEN
OLIVES, QUARTERED OR
HALVED IF NOT VERY BIG

ABOUT 1 TEASPOON THYME
LEAVES, PLUS THYME SPRIGS TO
SCATTER ON TOP IF YOU LIKE

FRESHLY GROUND
BLACK PEPPER

Serves 6

*This is lovely with a nice big salad, as the start to a meal
or even a light lunch. I like the ham and green olives
together, but you really could add anything you like.*

Preheat the oven to 350°F. Butter a 9½-inch round
springform pan. On a large sheet of wax paper roll out the
pastry to a 13½-inch circle. Use to line the pan, with the
pastry coming two-thirds of the way up the side.

Whip the eggs in a bowl, then mix in the cream,
Parmesan, ham, olives, and thyme. Add a few grindings of
black pepper and mix it all well. Scrape out into the pastry,
pushing the ham and olives around with the tip of a spoon
to fill any empty spaces. Bake for about 35 minutes, or
until the top is golden here and there, and set. Don't
overcook it, but make sure the pastry is golden around
the edges, well cooked, and crisp underneath.

Let cool a bit before cutting. I like this tart warm but it
can also be eaten at room temperature.

PAN DI ROSMARINO

◇◇

¼ OUNCES FRESH YEAST OR 2
TEASPOONS ACTIVE DRY YEAST

½ TEASPOON RUNNY HONEY

1 CUP TEPID WATER

3⅓ CUPS BREAD FLOUR

1 TEASPOON SALT

2 EGGS

2½ TABLESPOONS OLIVE OIL

⅔ CUP ZIBBIBO RAISINS (SEE
GLOSSARY, PAGE 329) OR
SMALL SEEDLESS MUSCATELS

5 TABLESPOONS
CHOPPED ROSEMARY

FRESHLY GROUND
BLACK PEPPER

*Makes 9 panini or
1 big loaf*

*These are flavorsome small rolls, full of raisins and rosemary.
They are typical of Florence and are great simply plain as a
snack (or merenda, as they say in Italy). I also like them toasted
with a nice mature pecorino or goat's cheese. Toasted and
spread with butter and jam is delicious, too.*

Crumble or place the yeast into a large bowl. Add the honey,
water, and a large handful of flour. Whisk until smooth, then set
aside until the yeast begins to activate. Add the rest of the flour,
the salt, and one of the eggs, whisked lightly. Mix until a dough
forms, then knead with floured hands on a lightly floured surface
until smooth and compact, adding a little more flour or water if
necessary. Return to the bowl, mark a cross in the top, and cover
with a kitchen towel. Leave in a warm place for about an hour to
puff up.

   Put the olive oil and raisins in a small saucepan. Gently sauté
until the raisins have absorbed most of the oil, have plumped up,
and are a bit golden. Add the rosemary, along with six or seven
good grinds of black pepper, and stir until it is heated through
and smells good. Remove from the heat and leave to cool.

   When the dough has risen, remove it to a lightly floured work
surface. Add the raisin mixture and knead until incorporated.
Divide the dough into nine portions and shape each into a
smooth round ball. If you prefer, you can leave it as one large
loaf. Put on a baking sheet lined with waxed paper, with space in
between for spreading, and leave to rise, covered, for 35 to 40
minutes.

   Preheat the oven to 350°F. Whisk the remaining egg and
brush gently over the top of each ball of dough, then scatter
a little fine salt over them. Bake for 20 to 25 minutes, until
golden on the top and bottom. A large loaf may need up to 10
minutes longer in the oven. The rolls can be frozen once cooled
completely.

SNACK

BOX

GRILLED CUTTLEFISH & ZUCCHINI

NEW GARLIC OMELET

OMELET WITH BLOSSOMS

FRIED ACACIA BLOSSOMS

CROSTINI WITH ANCHOVY,
SUN-DRIED TOMATO & MASCARPONE

MARISA'S PUMPKIN CROSTONE

TOMATO, MOZZARELLA
& HERB BRUSCHETTA

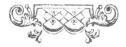

No. 322. 1s.

04 *The* 11

SNACK

BOX

THE SMALL THINGS

*Isn't it lovely how the
casalinga Italiana has
such a knack …*

TO SPREAD OUT A MEAL
SO SMOOTHLY AND SO FLUENTLY.
TO TURN OUT AN ANTIPASTO—A
NIBBLE HERE AND THERE.
TO SLIP IN AN EXTRA LAYER WITH
BITS AND PIECES TAKEN FROM
THIS AND THAT. A SMALL CROSTINO,
AN EGG, A FEW SLIVERS OF
BUTTER AND ANCHOVIES …
TO MAKE PEOPLE HAPPY.

GRILLED CUTTLEFISH & ZUCCHINI

14 OUNCES SMALL TO
MEDIUM CUTTLEFISH

2 WHOLE MEDIUM CLOVES
GARLIC, PEELED

5 TABLESPOONS OLIVE OIL

JUICE OF 1 LEMON

PINCH OF GROUND CHILE

1 TEASPOON DRIED OREGANO

3 ZUCCHINI, CUT
DIAGONALLY INTO ROUNDS
OF 1¼ TO 1½ INCHES

1 HEAPING TABLESPOON
CHOPPED PARSLEY

SMALL FISTFUL OF
BASIL LEAVES

SALT AND FRESHLY
GROUND BLACK PEPPER

Serves 6 as an antipasto

This is a lovely antipasto that could be followed by a whole broiled or roasted fish, for example. On the other hand, it could also make a light summer lunch on its own. It's great warm, but also good at room temperature.

Clean the cuttlefish. Remove the ink sac, cut off the wings and reserve, then remove the beaky part around the tentacles and discard. Pull out and discard the quill. Leave the tentacles whole, or halve if big. Open out the body and slash it on the inside (not all the way through) so it won't curl horizontally during cooking.

Squash a clove garlic with a large knife and combine with 2½ tablespoons of olive oil, the lemon juice, and the chile. Crumble in the oregano and season with salt and pepper.

Heat the remaining 2½ tablespoons of olive oil in a large nonstick skillet, add the other whole clove of garlic and the zucchini and sauté until the zucchini is nicely colored and cooked through, but not soggy. Toss the pan now and then to turn the zucchini. Season with salt and pepper.

Put a grill pan over high heat and when it's very hot, add the cuttlefish steaks, and the tentacles and wings on the sides. Cook until they turn opaque and golden marks appear underneath, then turn and cook the other side. Transfer to a board and scatter with a little salt. Slice up the steaks and tentacles into strips of about ¼ inch. Arrange the zucchini on your serving plate and then layer the cuttlefish on top. Scatter with the parsley and tear the basil on top. Drizzle the top with the dressing. Give a final grind or two of black pepper. Serve immediately or leave for a while for the flavors to mingle. Serve with bread.

SAPIENTE

WORDS/PAROLE

YOU CAN'T MAKE AN OMELET
WITHOUT BREAKING THE EGGS.

2½ TABLESPOONS
RINSED, ROUGHLY SLICED
NEW GARLIC, WHITE
WITH SOME GREEN

1 TABLESPOON + 1
TEASPOON OLIVE OIL

1 EGG

SALT AND FRESHLY
GROUND BLACK PEPPER

Serves 1

NEW GARLIC OMELET

Nonna said she went to see a woman in the countryside who asked her at the last minute to stay to lunch. She then dashed into her field to collect some new garlic in its brief season. Nonna said it was the best omelet she'd tasted, yet with almost nothing in it—just the contadina's *eggs and garlic. You just need a piece of bread on the side and you can add Parmesan to serve, if you like. It is lovely, simple, and pure.*

In a small nonstick skillet of about 5 inches that has a lid, sauté the garlic very gently in the olive oil. Add just a few grains of salt and stir so it doesn't get dark in any places but just softens and turns golden. Whip the egg in a bowl with a pinch of salt.

Pour the egg over the evenly distributed garlic and cook on a high heat at first, using a wooden spatula to push down any sides that have swayed up. Turn the heat right down and cover with a lid, cooking until the omelet is just set but still a little creamy on top. If you feel it is getting too dark underneath and the top is not yet set, you can turn off the heat and leave the lid on for half a minute or so, but don't leave it too long or it can become rubbery. It must still be creamy on top. Serve at once with a grind of pepper and a little extra salt sprinkled on top if needed.

HANDFUL OF EDIBLE SMALL
UNSPRAYED FLOWERS OR
PETALS SUCH AS ACACIA
(ROBINA PSEUDOACACI),
SAMBUCO/ELDERFLOWER,
VIOLETS, ROSES

1 EGG

A LITTLE OLIVE OIL

1 HEAPING TABLESPOON
SHREDDED PARMESAN,
PLUS EXTRA, TO SERVE

FRESHLY GROUND PINK
PEPPERCORNS, TO SERVE

Serves 1

OMELET WITH BLOSSOMS

A lovely springtime dish to add a splash of color and health.

If necessary, rinse the petals very gently and pat them dry. Halve them if they are big and remove any inner parts. Whip the egg in a small bowl. Heat a splash of oil in a 5-inch nonstick skillet that has a lid and swirl it around so the bottom is covered.

Pour in the egg, using a wooden spatula to push down any sides that have swayed up. Turn the heat right down. Scatter the Parmesan over the top and as soon as it starts to melt, scatter the blossoms over. Cover with a lid for a few moments to just set them in, so the egg remains creamy on top. Serve at once with a grind of pink pepper and extra Parmesan if you like.

FRIED ACACIA BLOSSOMS

When acacia blossoms (see Glossary, page 328) appear on the trees you shouldn't delay, as the season comes and goes very quickly. This is lovely served with an aperitif of prosecco or white wine, or alongside a main course. When panfried, they have a crisp, fresh, slightly sweet taste. Make sure the acacia blossoms you get are the edible type, as they can vary from place to place. The botanical name of the edible variety is Robina pseudoacaci.

Collect sprigs of acacia when the flowers are plump and fresh, not drying out on their branches. Make up a loose batter with an egg, flour, a little milk, and a pinch of salt. Dip the flowers in the batter, letting the excess drip away.

Heat some light olive oil in a skillet. Fry the slim sprigs until golden, then drain on paper towels. Serve hot and strip away at the fried flowers with your teeth.

CROSTINI WITH ANCHOVY, SUN-DRIED TOMATO & MASCARPONE

THE
LIST

2½ TABLESPOONS
SLICED RED ONION

SPLASH OF RED WINE VINEGAR

1 OUNCE SUN-DRIED TOMATOES
(NOT PACKED IN OIL)

4 TABLESPOONS OLIVE OIL

8 ANCHOVY FILLETS,
CHOPPED COARSELY

1 HEAPING TABLESPOON
CHOPPED PARSLEY

1 TEASPOON FINELY
CHOPPED ROSEMARY

5 SLICES COUNTRY-STYLE
BREAD, ROUGHLY 2½
INCHES IN DIAMETER

ABOUT 4 TABLESPOONS
MASCARPONE

Makes 5

I love starting a meal with a small bite of something interesting, such as this. Italians always do this sort of thing well and it takes the meal to a different level. It's quite possible that you will have all the ingredients at home already, apart from the mascarpone perhaps.

Soak the onion in cold water with the splash of vinegar for 20 minutes or so. At the same time, soak the sun-dried tomatoes in warm water to plump them up.

Drain the tomatoes and chop them into quite large, long pieces. Put them in a bowl with the olive oil. Drain the onion and add to the bowl, along with the anchovies, parsley, rosemary, and a few grinds of black pepper. Broil the bread. Roughly spread a couple of teaspoons of mascarpone over each crostino, then top with the anchovy mixture and serve.

2¼ POUNDS WINTER SQUASH

4 TABLESPOONS OLIVE OIL,
PLUS EXTRA, FOR DRIZZLING

⅔ CUP CHOPPED WHITE ONION

10 TO 12 SAGE LEAVES

6 SLICES COUNTRY-STYLE BREAD

1 WHOLE MEDIUM CLOVE
GARLIC, PEELED

3 TABLESPOONS BUTTER

8 TABLESPOONS
SHREDDED PARMESAN

SALT AND FRESHLY
GROUND BLACK PEPPER

Makes 6

MARISA'S WINTER SQUASH CROSTONE

This is lovely and really easy as a starter. And such a simple way to slide an extra vegetable into a meal.

Peel the winter squash, remove the seeds, and cut it into large chunks. Heat the olive oil in a large saucepan and sauté the onion until pale golden and soft. Add a couple of the sage leaves and cook for a minute to flavor, then add the winter squash, 1 cup of water and some salt and pepper. Put on the lid and simmer for 30 to 40 minutes, until the pumpkin has collapsed. Check now and then that nothing is sticking or it doesn't need a few more drops of water. Taste for salt.

Grill the bread. Lightly rub one side of each piece with garlic and drizzle a little olive oil over. Top with a good heap of warm winter squash. Put the remaining sage leaves and the butter in a small saucepan and heat until the sage is crisp and the butter is golden. If the butter is getting too dark before the sage is crisp, add a little more to the pan. Drizzle the butter over the winter squash, scatter the Parmesan and crisp sage leaves on top, and give a good grind of black pepper. Serve hot.

SAPIENTE
WORDS/PAROLE

WILMA ASSIGNED A COLOR
TO EACH OF HER SONS.
GIOVANNI WAS GREEN AND
HAD A GREEN LOOP ON HIS
TOWELS, A GREEN THREAD
SEWN IN HIS JEANS ... THIS
MADE WASHING DAY
MUCH EASIER

TOMATO, MOZZARELLA & HERB BRUSCHETTA

THE
LIST

2 SLICES
COUNTRY-STYLE
BREAD

1 WHOLE MEDIUM CLOVE GARLIC,
PEELED

ABOUT 4 TABLESPOONS
OLIVE OIL

4 THICK LARGE SLICES
OF TOMATO

½ TABLESPOON
CHOPPED OREGANO

½-INCH-THICK SLICES
FRESH MOZZARELLA

SMALL FISTFUL OF
BASIL LEAVES

SALT AND FRESHLY
GROUND BLACK PEPPER

Serves 2

Simplicity. This is a quick pizza really, a delicious snack that you can throw together in a moment.

Preheat the oven to 425°F.

Toast the bread directly on the oven rack until both sides are just lightly golden. Rub garlic over one side of each slice, then put on a baking sheet and drizzle 1 generous tablespoon of olive oil over each. Cover each with two slices of tomato, then a little drizzle of oil, and season with salt and a few grinds of pepper. Scatter some of the oregano on top, then top with the mozzarella slices and the rest of the oregano. Put in the oven and bake until the mozzarella starts to melt. Put on plates, give a final drizzle of olive oil, and scatter the basil leaves on top. Give one or two grinds of black pepper and serve at once.

— THE —

Vegetable Patch

ARTICHOKE & MINT SOUP

TOMATO SOUP WITH RICE & BASIL

AUTUMN VEGETABLE SOUP

VEGETABLES WITH "BAGNA CAUDA"

RADICCHIO & APPLE SALAD

GREEN SALAD

MARTA'S MOM'S FENNEL

MARISA'S POTATOES WITH CRUMBS

SAUTÉED ARTICHOKES
& POTATOES

SALT & PEPPER POTATOES WITH
A TRICKLE OF BUTTERMILK

SALT & BALSAMIC VINEGAR

SAUTÉED POTATOES

SAUTÉED CARDOONS
WITH PARMESAN

ZUCCHINI & FLOWERS

MARIELLA'S ZUCCHINI

No.
5

WE ASKED FOR CAVOLO NERO AT THE
MARKET AND THE *FRUTTIVENDOLO* SAID
TO COME BACK – WHEN WE HAD OUR
WARM WINTER COATS ON, THEN THE
CAVOLO NERO WOULD BE READY.

ARTICHOKE & MINT SOUP

This is a good and healthful bowlful of soup for a primo. Be sure to include some of the artichoke stems as they, too, are rich in iron. Have a bowl of water with some lemon squeezed in on the side to keep the outer artichoke leaves that you strip away and would otherwise discard. (Later you can dip the tender bottoms of these leaves in olive oil and a little salt as a snack.) I like to serve this soup with small squares of bread panfried in olive oil until golden.

Put the potatoes, onion, celery, carrot, 6 cups of water and olive oil in a large pot. Season with salt and bring to a boil.

Meanwhile, clean the artichokes. Cut off the stems and strip away the outer woody part of each until you reach the paler tender part. Chop these up and put in the pot. Now strip away the outer leaves from the artichokes until you reach the more tender inner ones, then cut off and discard the top third of each. Now is a good time to taste a leaf and check you've gone far enough in to be able to eat the whole leaf without having any fibrous bits left in your mouth. Cut the artichokes in half, then cut out and discard the hairy choke. Give the artichokes a quick rinse and then chop up into large chunks directly into the pot.

Cover and simmer for 30 minutes, or until the vegetables are tender. Using a handheld blender, puree until completely smooth. Check that the consistency is good, adding a little hot water if it seems too thick. Taste for salt. Serve hot, with an extra drizzle of olive oil, some grated Parmesan, a few grinds of black pepper, and the mint leaves torn over each bowl.

TOMATO SOUP WITH RICE & BASIL

5 TABLESPOONS OLIVE OIL, PLUS EXTRA, FOR SERVING

1 SMALL RED ONION, CHOPPED

2 MEDIUM CLOVES GARLIC, CHOPPED

1¾ POUNDS VERY RIPE TOMATOES, PEELED AND CHOPPED

12–15 BASIL LEAVES

5 CUPS HOT WATER

1 SCANT CUP SHORT-GRAIN WHITE RICE

8 TO 10 TABLESPOONS GRATED PARMESAN, TO SERVE

Serves 5 or 6

This is simple and summery, just the thing for when you have beautiful ripe tomatoes in your vegetable patch. How can it not be great, with tomatoes, basil, olive oil, and garlic?

Heat the olive oil in a large pot and sauté the onion until nicely golden and a bit sticky. Add the garlic and when it smells great, add the tomatoes. Bring to a boil and season with salt and pepper. Tear in about seven of the basil leaves and simmer for 5 minutes or so, squashing down most of the tomato lumps with a potato masher. Add the hot water and simmer, covered, for about 20 minutes.

Add the rice and simmer for another 20 minutes or so, putting the lid on at the end to prevent too much liquid from evaporating. It should be quite thick, but if it seems too thick just add a little hot water. Taste for seasoning and adjust if necessary.

Serve in wide bowls. Tear a couple of basil leaves in half and add to each bowl. Scatter a heaping tablespoon or so of Parmesan over each and drizzle with a little olive oil. Grind a little black pepper over the top and serve.

AUTUMN VEGETABLE SOUP

Serves 6 to 8

*This is a huge, warm and friendly pot of everything.
It would be made when the new extra-virgin olive oil of the
season is ready and this would be used during the cooking
and also drizzled over the soup just before serving. You
need a big pot, of course. You can vary the vegetables,
but whatever you use should be cut up irregularly so
they're all different, rather than an army of the same.
I like to cook the cranberry beans in a pressure cooker.*

Drain the water from the borlotti beans after soaking
overnight. Put the beans in a pot, cover with plenty of fresh
water and add a whole clove garlic and the sage leaves.
Bring to a boil, cover, and simmer over low heat for
1 hour or as long as necessary, until the beans are tender.
Check now and then that there is an abundant amount of
water covering the beans. Add salt only toward the end
of the cooking time. Take off the heat, but don't drain.

To prepare the cavolo nero, hold each stalk at its base
and use your other hand to strip the leaf off. Shred the
leaves and discard the stalks.

Meanwhile, heat the olive oil in a large, wide pot and
sauté the onion and leek until lightly golden. Add the
chopped garlic and sauté for a moment. Add the celery
and carrot and sauté for a while longer. Stir with a wooden
spoon. Add the potatoes, cabbage, and cavolo nero,
season with salt and a little pepper and add 6 cups of
water. Bring to a boil, then lower the heat and simmer,
partly covered, until the vegetables are lovely and tender,
about 1 hour 15 minutes. Add 2 cups of water as the soup
thickens, about halfway through the cooking time.

Drain the borlotti beans, keeping the cooking broth.
Puree 1 cup of the beans with 2 cups of the broth. Add
to the pot with the whole beans and simmer for another
15 minutes or so to blend all of the flavors. If it seems too
thick, add a little more of the bean broth. Remove from
the heat and let rest, covered.

Broil the bread. Rub one side gently with the remaining
clove of garlic, then drizzle a little olive oil over each slice.
Ladle the soup into bowls and top each with a good
drizzle of olive oil, a grind of pepper and a scattering of
chili powder. You can decide whether you would like this
with grated Parmesan or without.

VEGETABLES WITH "BAGNA CAUDA"

5½ OUNCES ANCHOVIES IN SALT

1½ CUPS MILK

ABOUT 10 MEDIUM CLOVES
GARLIC, COARSELY CHOPPED

9 TABLESPOONS OLIVE OIL,
PLUS A LITTLE EXTRA

PINCH OF CHILI POWDER

YOUR CHOICE OF VEGETABLES

HARD-COOKED EGGS

TOASTED SLICES OF
COUNTRY-STYLE BREAD

ROSEMARY LEAVES

FRESHLY GROUND BLACK
PEPPER

Serves 4

This can stand alone as a main meal, but would also be good before a broiled fish dish. It is from northern Italy, where the sauce is traditionally kept warm over a flame so the vegetables can be dipped in it as everybody talks the night away. Here I have made a sauce to serve with a platter of vegetables. You can use any vegetables of your choice. The kind of anchovies to use are those whole ones packed in salt, which usually come in beautiful huge cans.

Rinse the anchovies and fillet them, removing the central bone. Put in a bowl and cover with ½ cup of the milk. Leave to soak for half an hour or so. Meanwhile, in a medium saucepan, sauté the garlic in 5 tablespoons of the olive oil until it smells good. Add the remaining milk and simmer, partly covered and stirring regularly so the garlic doesn't stick, for 20 minutes or so, until pulpy.

When the garlic is very soft, mash it into the milk in the saucepan with a potato masher or fork until pureed. Drain the anchovies, discarding the milk, then pat dry with paper towels and chop them up finely. Add to the garlic puree in the saucepan, along with the remaining 4 tablespoons of olive oil and a good grind of black pepper. Simmer, stirring very regularly, for about 10 minutes. Remove from the heat and stir in the chili powder and extra olive oil, if needed.

Prepare your accompaniments while the sauce is cooking. For example, boil potatoes in salted water, blanch cauliflower florets, or hard-cook a couple of eggs. Rinse and trim scallions, carrots, inner celery stalks with some leaves, fennel, red peppers, artichokes. Rinse tomatoes, radishes, green radicchio leaves. Grill a few slices of bread. Chop enough rosemary leaves to fill a small plate. Arrange them all on platters or suitable serving dishes and serve with the sauce, which must be served warm with an extra grind of black pepper.

RADICCHIO & APPLE SALAD

¾ OUNCE SHALLOT

SPLASH OF WINE VINEGAR

½ RED APPLE (I LIKE THE FUJI VARIETY HERE), UNPEELED

1 TO 2 TEASPOONS FRESHLY SQUEEZED LEMON JUICE

2¾ OUNCES RED RADICCHIO LEAVES

6 WALNUT HALVES

1 TEASPOON CHESTNUT HONEY

4 TABLESPOONS OLIVE OIL

1 TABLESPOON + 1 TEASPOON BALSAMIC VINEGAR

ABOUT 1½ OUNCES SHAVED MATURE PECORINO OR PARMESAN

SALT AND FRESHLY GROUND BLACK PEPPER

Serves 2

I love a salad like this—full of color, crunch and flavor, yet so simple to put together. It has a rather strong autumnal feel. This is about strewing good ingredients onto a plate and reaping the benefits in the overall flavor and freshness.

Thinly slice the shallot and put in a small bowl of cold water with the vinegar (this helps to get rid of the acidity in the shallot). Leave to soak for 20 minutes or so. Cut the apple into 1/16 to 1/8-inch slices and put in a bowl of cold water with the lemon juice and a sprinkling of salt.

Cut away the thick white spine from the radicchio, then tear up or shred the leaves thickly. Divide between two plates and arrange in a nice heap. Shake the apple dry and arrange in and around the radicchio. Scatter a little salt on top, then break up the walnuts with your fingers and scatter on top. Drain and rinse the onion, pat dry with paper towel, and scatter over the salad.

For the dressing, put the honey in a small bowl and stir in the olive oil and balsamic vinegar with a little salt and pepper. Mix with a small whisk or fork to dissolve the honey, then drizzle over the salads. Scatter the pecorino on top, give a few grinds of black pepper, and serve.

SAPIENTE
WORDS/PAROLE

A HALVED ONION IS GOOD FOR
CLEANING GOLD AND SILVER
GILDED FRAMES, AND MAKING
THEM SHINE.

2¾ OUNCES TRIMMED SCALLION
WITH SOME GREEN PART

2¾ OUNCES INNER CELERY
STALKS WITH LEAVES

2¾ OUNCES CUCUMBER, PEELED

1½ OUNCES VALERIANA
(LAMB'S LETTUCE; SEE
GLOSSARY, PAGE 329)

1½ OUNCES ARUGULA

2 TABLESPOONS VERY
COARSELY CHOPPED PARSLEY

1 TABLESPOON OLIVE OIL

JUICE OF 1 SMALL LEMON

½ FULLY RIPE AVOCADO

SMALL HANDFUL OF
MINT LEAVES

SALT AND FRESHLY
GROUND BLACK PEPPER

Serves 4

GREEN SALAD

*I love this salad next to anything, even my bed!
I could eat it all day and never be tired, ever. It refreshes
and recharges me. If your arugula is large, tear it in half.
I only use a little oil as the lemon carries this salad along
and the avocado holds the richness. Needless to say,
your avocado must be a beauty—at full ripeness, but not
past this. It can make or break the situation. If valeriana is
unavailable, you could use picked watercress leaves.*

Rinse, dry, and chop the scallion, celery and cucumber
and put in a bowl with the *valeriana*, arugula and parsley.
Add a little salt and pepper. Mix the oil and lemon juice
together in a small bowl or cup with a little salt and
pepper. Pour over the salad and mix gently. Scoop chunks
of avocado into the salad, tear the mint leaves in, gently
stir again and serve soon.

MARTA'S MOM'S FENNEL

3 MEDIUM FENNEL
BULBS, TRIMMED

6 TABLESPOONS OLIVE OIL

2 WHOLE MEDIUM CLOVES
GARLIC, PEELED

1 (14-OUNCE) CAN
CHOPPED TOMATOES

4 BASIL LEAVES

ABOUT 3 TABLESPOONS
ALL-PURPOSE FLOUR

1 HEAPING TABLESPOON
DRIED BREAD CRUMBS

2½ TABLESPOONS
GRATED PARMESAN

SALT AND FRESHLY
GROUND BLACK PEPPER

Serves 6

This is from my friend Marta's mother. It's a wonderful way with fennel. She says that it is important to cook it for a long time so the fennel is given time to dry, to get it beyond the waterlogged aspect it can sometimes have. I use an oval ceramic dish to make these in, where the fennel fits compactly in a single layer. It is lovely with fish and meat, particularly pork.

Quarter the fennel bulbs from the top down, making sure the pieces stay hinged together. Bring a pot of salted water to a boil and cook the fennel for 10 minutes or so, until softened but not soggy and overdone. Test with a fork to see that it is tender. Drain in a colander and pat dry with paper towels.

Preheat the oven to 350°F.

Heat 3 tablespoons of the oil with one clove of garlic in a small pot until it smells good. Add the tomatoes with some salt and pepper, and simmer for 10 minutes or so, until it is a sauce. Tear in the basil just toward the end so it will perfume the tomato. Remove from the heat.

Use a large nonstick skillet for the fennel. Put the flour in a bowl and pat it onto the fennel, coating it on all sides. Heat the remaining 3 tablespoons of olive oil in the pan. Add the fennel, in one layer, and the other clove of garlic. Sauté the fennel until golden and firm on all sides. If the garlic browns, remove it as it will have done its job.

Dollop about half the tomato sauce here and there on the bottom of the baking dish that you'll bake the fennel in. Arrange the fennel in so it all fits compactly. If some of the pieces are very big, halve them. Dollop the rest of the tomato sauce on top. Scatter the bread crumbs and Parmesan on top, and bake for about 20 minutes, or until the top is golden and crusty in places. Serve warm. Also lovely at room temperature.

si fecero sempre...
fece annessi...
solo baccio...
qui suoi...
gli...
cure qualche...
ribare tutto...
libre velluttate...
Poss - ribe...
povero...
spezzato con...

...u odore, per ...

...talmente il ...bbo...

...ol eno ... ...giu fur...

...llutati ......

...re in boccia, muore

...di grande di al...

...u amore che tener...

...i suoi petali ro...

...con per l'ultima...

...bello, ed rosiur dolor...

...ene bufera strana...

MARISA'S POTATOES
WITH CRUMBS

ABOUT 2 POUNDS 10 OUNCES
POTATOES

9 TABLESPOONS OLIVE OIL

2 FISTFULS OF DRIED
BREAD CRUMBS

12 BIG SAGE LEAVES

SALT AND FRESHLY
GROUND BLACK PEPPER

Serves 6 or more

Everybody loves Nonna Marisa's potatoes. Marisa is always making brodo *and* sugo *and distributing them among her kin, in between doing their ironing and loving her grandchildren. It is important to use a nonstick baking dish for this.*

Preheat the oven to 400°F. Peel the potatoes and cut into chunks, not too big. Keep in a bowl of cold water until you are ready to cook them.

Pour half the olive oil onto the bottom of a nonstick baking dish, about 9 by 13 inches. Pour the potatoes into a colander and immediately scatter the bread crumbs so they'll stick to the clinging water. Stir once with your hands, then pour the potatoes and crumbs into the baking dish. Scatter with the sage leaves (torn in half if very big), and salt and pepper. Add the rest of the olive oil and toss quickly but thoroughly, making sure each potato is well coated.

Roast the potatoes for about 50 minutes, turning only after the bottoms are golden, about 35 minutes. Turn again until crusty and golden all over. Taste to check they have enough salt, then serve at once.

SAUTÉED ARTICHOKES & POTATOES

5 ARTICHOKES, WITH ABOUT 2½ INCHES STEM ATTACHED

JUICE OF 1 LEMON

5 TABLESPOONS OLIVE OIL

2 SCALLIONS, TRIMMED AND CHOPPED

14 OUNCES POTATOES, PEELED, HALVED AND SLICED INTO ⅛ INCH-ROUNDS

2 MEDIUM CLOVES GARLIC, CHOPPED

1 TEASPOON DRIED OREGANO

1 HEAPING TABLESPOON CHOPPED PARSLEY

SALT AND FRESHLY GROUND BLACK PEPPER

Serves 4 to 6

Trim away the outer dark green part of the artichoke stems to get to the paler inner part. Tear away the tough outer leaves to get to the tender inner ones that will not be fibrous in your mouth when cooked. Cut off the top third of the artichokes, then halve them lengthwise. Scoop out the hairy chokes with a small knife or teaspoon. Cut each half into four lengths, still attached at the stem. Put in a bowl of water with the lemon juice squeezed in and leave until you are ready for them.

Heat the oil in a wide nonstick skillet. Add the scallions and sauté a bit before adding the potatoes and drained artichokes. Sauté gently until a little golden here and there. Add the garlic and some salt and pepper and sauté a little more. Add ¼ cup of water and simmer, uncovered, for about 20 minutes, or until all are tender. Add the oregano and parsley and continue cooking until almost all the pan juices have been absorbed. Taste for seasoning, then serve.

SALT & PEPPER POTATOES WITH A TRICKLE OF BUTTERMILK

6 TO 8 MEDIUM POTATOES

ABOUT 8 TEASPOONS
PEPPER SALT (PAGE 25), PLUS
A LITTLE EXTRA, TO SERVE

ABOUT 11 TABLESPOONS
BUTTER (PAGE 328)

ABOUT 1½ CUPS BUTTERMILK

Serves 6 to 8

There's not much to this—just whole potatoes, scattered with a crunchy salt and pepper mix, then baked in foil. A blob of butter and a little buttermilk makes them soft and creamy. They are simple and so very good, especially with roasted meats. Have the butter and buttermilk at room temperature so they don't cool down the potatoes.

Preheat the oven to 400°F. Tear pieces of foil, each large enough to wrap a potato in, and put in a pile. Wash the potatoes well and scrub the skins. Hold each potato over a piece of foil, prick it here and there with a fork, and while still damp (so it sticks) scatter with a heaping teaspoon of the pepper salt. The amount you need will depend on the size of the potatoes.

Wrap up each potato in foil and put on a baking sheet. Bake for about 50 minutes, or until the potatoes surrender easily when pressed. Remove from the oven. Take a little extra pepper salt, and crush it a little finer to serve on the side. Serve the potatoes hot and still in the foil, for everyone to unwrap their own. They should be halved down the middle, pressed up from the bottom to fluff up, then topped with a blob of butter and a good trickle of buttermilk. Sprinkle the crushed pepper salt over the top.

SALT & BALSAMIC VINEGAR SAUTÉED POTATOES

SOME COARSE SALT

2¼ POUNDS POTATOES

5 TABLESPOONS OLIVE OIL

2 WHOLE MEDIUM CLOVES
GARLIC, PEELED

½ CUP BALSAMIC VINEGAR

2 SPRIGS ROSEMARY, PLUS
EXTRA, TO SERVE (OPTIONAL)

FRESHLY GROUND
BLACK PEPPER

Serves 6

These are easy to make and go well with a plain roasted meat. It's good to make a stovetop potato dish when your oven is full of roasting meat.

In a mortar, crush some coarse salt with a pestle to break it down a bit, but still leave some texture. Peel the potatoes, rinse them, halve lengthwise and cut into gondolas. Heat the olive oil in a large nonstick skillet that has a lid. Add the potatoes and garlic and sauté over a fairly high heat, turning through and tossing until they have a bit of color and are starting to stick. Season with some of the crushed salt and a little pepper. Add half the vinegar and turn through. Sit the rosemary sprigs on top, cover with a lid and lower the heat.

Simmer for about 15 minutes or so, until the potatoes are tender and much of the vinegar seems to have been absorbed. Add the rest of the vinegar, stir and cook, uncovered now, for 10 minutes, or until the potatoes are tender and crisping up just a bit and most of the liquid has reduced. Sprinkle with a little extra salt on and serve hot with a couple of extra rosemary sprigs on top if you like. These are also surprisingly good at room temperature.

SAUTÉED CARDOONS WITH PARMESAN

2 LEMONS

2 POUNDS 10 OUNCES
CARDOONS (SEE
GLOSSARY, PAGE 328)

5 TABLESPOONS OLIVE OIL

2 WHOLE MEDIUM CLOVES
GARLIC, PEELED

GOOD PINCH OF CHILI POWDER

8 TABLESPOONS
GRATED PARMESAN

SALT AND FRESHLY
GROUND BLACK PEPPER

—

Serves 4 to 6

I like to serve this elegant dish with roast guinea fowl or lamb. The cardoons have a bitter yet beautiful flavor that stays with you. The work involved in stripping and cleaning them is well worth it. Wilma says that when boiling cardoons, one can put a clean kitchen towel over them in the water to make sure they are all immersed. Cardoons, like artichokes, are very good for you. If cardoons are not available, you could use thistles instead.

Have a bowl of cold water ready with the juice of one lemon squeezed in. If the cardoons are attached, separate the stalks from the base. Leave the tender very inner stalks whole with their leaves attached (cook them with the rest, then eat them with some oil and lemon juice). Wearing gloves and using a small, sharp knife or potato peeler, strip away the outer strings of the stalks by digging in at one end of the stalk and dragging all the way down. The strings are unpleasant to eat so make sure you get all of them. As you work, cut the stalks into irregular lengths of 2½ or 2¾ inches and drop them into the lemon water so they don't darken. Make sure they are submerged.

Bring a pot of salted water to a boil. Add the drained cardoons and squeeze in the juice of the remaining lemon. Boil, uncovered, for about 35 minutes or until the cardoons are tender when poked with a fork. You may need to remove the thinner stalks if they are cooked before the rest are ready. Drain well.

Heat the oil in a large nonstick skillet and add the cardoons, garlic, chili powder, and salt and pepper. Sauté until golden here and there, about 15 minutes or longer if necessary. Remove from the heat, scatter the Parmesan over the top, and put the lid on for a few minutes so the cheese melts into the cardoons. Serve warm.

ZUCCHINI & FLOWERS

7 ZUCCHINI, WITH
FLOWERS ATTACHED

10 OR SO ZUCCHINI
FLOWERS, EXTRA

1 SMALL RED ONION, CHOPPED

5 TABLESPOONS OLIVE OIL

2 MEDIUM CLOVES
GARLIC, CHOPPED

1 (14-OUNCE) CAN
CHOPPED TOMATOES

FISTFUL OF BASIL
LEAVES, TORN

SALT AND FRESHLY
GROUND BLACK PEPPER

Serves 6

This is a great two-in-one recipe. The dark green outer part of the zucchini is stripped off and can be served as part of an antipasto (see below) or with a main course. Use zucchini that aren't too big in diameter.

Remove the flowers attached to the zucchini and put with the extra flowers. Rinse the zucchini. Peel away the dark green outer part in long strips (use in the recipe below). Slice the zucchini into ⅝-inch slices. Sauté the onion in the oil in a wide pan until golden and cooked, then add the garlic. Sauté for a moment and when it smells good, add the tomatoes. Turn through and cook for a few minutes before adding the zucchini slices. Season with salt and pepper and add ½ cup of water, which you can first swish around in the tomato can. Cover and simmer for 20 minutes or so, until the zucchini is tender.

Meanwhile, open up the zucchini flowers and remove all the inner parts, discarding those. Rinse the flowers gently and pat dry with paper towels. Shred each into two or three pieces. Add the flowers and basil to the pan, stir through, and continue cooking, covered, for 10 minutes or so. If the sauce looks too thick, add a few drops of hot water, but it is a side dish, not a soup! Remove from the heat and leave with the lid on for 10 minutes or so, or until you serve them. These are also nice at room temperature.

MARIELLA'S ZUCCHINI

THE
LIST

ZUCCHINI STRIPS (SEE ABOVE)

4 TABLESPOONS OLIVE OIL

½ TEASPOON FINELY
GRATED LEMON ZEST,
YELLOW PART ONLY

JUICE OF ½ LEMON

SMALL HANDFUL OF MINT LEAVES

SALT AND FRESHLY
GROUND BLACK PEPPER

Serves 4 to 6

Mariella, a wonderful housewife and cook, taught me this. It's easy and such a good idea for using zucchini in a different way.

Put the zucchini strips in a bowl with the oil, lemon zest and juice, salt and pepper. Tear in the mint and stir to combine. Cover and put in the fridge for an hour or so before serving. Lovely even the next day.

The Pasta Pot

POTATO & TRUFFLE PURSES

RAVIOLI WITH ASPARAGUS, RICOTTA,
SAGE & BROWN BUTTER

BARBARA'S ASPARAGUS & HAM LASAGNA

PASTA AL FORNO SICILIANA

PENNE WITH CALAMARI, ZUCCHINI
& THEIR FLOWERS

SPAGHETTI WITH LENTIL RAGÙ

RAGÙ WITH MILK & GREEN TAGLIATELLE

GREEN TAGLIATELLE

SPAGHETTI WITH PANCETTA, PECORINO
& ROSEMARY CRUMBS

SPAGHETTI AGLIO, OLIO, PEPERONCINO
& AVOCADO

GIOVANNA'S SPAGHETTI

SPAGHETTI WITH CLAMS, TOMATO
& A DASH OF CREAM

SPAGHETTI WITH CLAMS & TABASCO

TORTA DI SPAGHETTI

BARBARA'S MUM'S SPINACH POLPETTINE

RISOTTO WITH SHRIMP,
LAVENDER & LEMON

RISOTTO WITH PEARS & PECORINO

QUICK VEGETABLE BROTH

The HOUSE Rules

3

USE LARGE WIDE PASTA BOWLS THAT YOU CAN TURN THE
PASTA AROUND IN, AND IF POSSIBLE, HAVE THEM WARM.

DO NOT PUT THE PASTA ON TO BOIL UNTIL ALL
THE DINERS HAVE ARRIVED.

PEOPLE SHOULD COME IMMEDIATELY WHEN THE COOK
CALLS, AS CLUMPING PASTA IS UNACCEPTABLE.

ABOUT 2 TEASPOONS OF SALT SHOULD BE ADDED FOR
10 CUPS OF WATER.

KEEP A RULE THAT YOU ALWAYS FOLLOW AS TO WHEN
YOU ADD THE SALT, TO AVOID NO SALT IN THE PASTA
OR TWICE-SALTED PASTA.

REGOLE

POTATO & TRUFFLE PURSES

THE
LIST

PASTA

1⅓ CUPS
ALL-PURPOSE FLOUR

2 EGGS, LIGHTLY BEATEN

1 TEASPOON OLIVE OIL

1 TEASPOON SALT

FILLING

1 POUND 2 OUNCES POTATOES

2½ TABLESPOONS
SHREDDED PARMESAN

ABOUT 1 TABLESPOON
TRUFFLE BUTTER (PAGE 19)

SALT AND FRESHLY GROUND
BLACK PEPPER

TO SERVE

2 OUTER LEEK JACKETS,
ABOUT 14¼ INCHES LONG

ABOUT 11 TABLESPOONS BUTTER

A WHITE TRUFFLE

SHREDDED PARMESAN, TO SERVE

Serves 6

I like to use white truffles here. The purses are not hard to make, just a bit time consuming. You will need a pasta machine to roll out the pasta. You'll also need long, thin ribbons of leek to hold the purses closed. If you can't get fresh truffles, you can use truffle butter or a few drops of truffle oil. It's worth noting that truffles vary in strength.

To make the pasta, mix the flour, eggs, olive oil, and salt in a bowl until the mixture comes together. Turn out and knead well until you have a lovely, soft dough. Cover with a kitchen towel and leave at room temperature to rest for about half an hour or so.

Meanwhile, make the filling. Boil the potatoes in their skins in boiling salted water until soft. At the same time, drop in the leek jackets and boil for a couple of minutes, until tender. Remove, drain, and put aside until cool enough to handle. Peel the potatoes while they are still hot by spiking a fork into each and dragging the skin off with a knife, using your other hand. Put in a bowl and mash with a potato masher, adding the Parmesan, truffle butter, and a little salt and pepper if needed. When the leek jackets have cooled, spread them on a board. Standing up so you can see better, cut them into long, thin ribbons, a couple of fractions of an inch wide.

Roll out about one-fifth of the dough, keeping the rest covered with a kitchen towel so it doesn't dry out. Feed the rolled dough through the highest setting on a pasta machine. Fold it up again like a book to neaten it and pass it through this setting again. Now pass it through the next setting twice, and so on until you are 3 notches from the

SAPIENTE
WORDS/PAROLE

finest setting. You can now cut the dough in half to make it more manageable if you like. You want the finished sheet of pasta straight-edged so fold the ends in to straighten, if necessary. Pass through this setting twice, then continue like this until you have used the finest setting and the length of pasta is as wide as the machine allows, with smooth straight edges all around. Proceed with the rest of the dough, keeping the rolled sheets covered with a kitchen towel so they don't dry out.

Cut the pasta sheets into squares of about 5 inches and keep covered. Working in batches of five or so, put about a tablespoon of filling into the middle of a square. Gently draw up the edges to bunch around the filling, being careful not to squash the pasta ruffles.

Tie up, using a leek ribbon, wrapping it around twice and then tying a knot gently so it doesn't snap. Line up the purses on a tray dusted with a little flour while you finish filling the rest. You will have about twenty purses.

Bring a low-sided, wide pot of salted water to a boil. Gently lower some of the purses into the water (don't overcrowd the pot) and simmer for about 5 minutes, or until tender. Don't boil rapidly or they may tear. Transfer with a slotted spoon to a warm dish while you cook the rest.

Meanwhile, melt the butter to just pale golden. Serve three purses per person in warm, wide bowls. Drizzle about 2 tablespoons of butter over each bowl, then shave some truffle over the top. Serve at once with a good scattering of Parmesan and a grind of pepper.

RAVIOLI WITH ASPARAGUS, RICOTTA, SAGE & BROWN BUTTER

PASTA

1⅓ CUPS ALL-PURPOSE FLOUR

2 EGGS, LIGHTLY BEATEN

1 TEASPOON OLIVE OIL

1 TEASPOON SALT

14 OUNCES ASPARAGUS

4 TABLESPOONS OLIVE OIL

¾ CUP CHOPPED SCALLIONS
WITH SOME GREEN PART

2½ TABLESPOONS
SHREDDED PARMESAN, PLUS
EXTRA, FOR SERVING

9 OUNCES FRESH RICOTTA

8 TABLESPOONS BUTTER

ABOUT 20 SAGE LEAVES

SALT AND FRESHLY
GROUND BLACK PEPPER

Serves 6 or more

This is beautiful. And see how easy it is to make a batch of homemade pasta? It's only 2 eggs and 1⅓ cups of flour, so you don't need everyone in the family and neighborhood to help roll it out and your house won't be crammed full of drying pasta.

To make the pasta, mix the flour, eggs, olive oil, and salt in a bowl until the mixture comes together. Turn out and knead well until you have a lovely, soft dough. Cover with a kitchen towel and leave at room temperature to rest for about half an hour or so.

Meanwhile, make the filling, as it will need time to cool down. Snap off and discard the woody ends of the asparagus. Cut off the tips (about 1½ inches) and keep them aside for now. Roughly chop up the rest. Heat the oil in a skillet and sauté the scallions until pale gold and softened. Add the chopped asparagus. Sauté, adding a little salt, until tender. Transfer to a bowl to cool. When completely cool, add the Parmesan and ricotta and mix well. Taste, adding salt and pepper if needed.

Roll out about one-fifth of the dough, keeping the rest covered with a kitchen towel so it doesn't dry out. Feed the rolled dough through the highest setting on a pasta machine. Fold it up again like a book to neaten it and pass it through this setting again. Now pass it through the next setting twice, and so on until you are three notches from the finest setting. You can now cut the dough in half to make it more manageable if you like. You want the finished sheet of pasta straight-edged, so fold the ends in to straighten, if necessary. Pass it through this setting twice, then continue like this until you have used the finest setting and the length of pasta is as wide as the machine allows, with smooth straight edges all around. Proceed with the rest of the dough, keeping the rolled sheets covered with a kitchen towel so they don't dry out.

Put a pasta sheet on a wooden board. Dollop

teaspoons of filling in a row about 1¼ inches in from one long side and with about 1¼ inches between each. If the pasta is drying out a bit, you may need to brush around the filling with a little water so the two layers of pasta will stick together. Carefully fold the other side over to cover the hills of filling. Press between each one to seal. Cut with a sharp knife between the hills and press firmly with the tines of a fork on the 3 sides that aren't folded. The ravioli should be about 2¾ by 2 inches but they don't have to be exact. Put them on a lightly floured tray while you make the rest.

Bring a low-sided, wide pot of salted water to a boil. Cook the ravioli, in batches, over not-too-high heat for about 5 minutes or until tender. Transfer with a slotted spoon to a warm dish while you cook the rest.

While the ravioli are cooking, heat three-quarters of the butter in a pan with the sage leaves and asparagus tips and sauté until the asparagus are a bit golden, the sage is crisp, and the butter is golden brown. When the butter starts to brown, add the rest to the pan to slow down the process so the sage has time to crisp up. Divide the ravioli among warm plates—five per person is a good amount. Divide the asparagus and sage among the plates and spoon some warm butter over each. Scatter Parmesan on top, give a grind of black pepper, and serve at once.

These can be frozen, uncooked, in individual layers on a tray so they don't all stick together. Once frozen, snap them off and store in the freezer in plastic bags.

BARBARA'S ASPARAGUS & HAM LASAGNA

2¼ POUNDS ASPARAGUS

2½ TABLESPOONS OLIVE OIL

½ CUP CHOPPED SCALLIONS
WITH SOME GREEN PART

2 TABLESPOONS
CHOPPED PARSLEY

6 SHEETS (6 BY 8¼ INCHES)
FRESH LASAGNA NOODLES,
ABOUT ½ POUND

ABOUT 6 TABLESPOONS
SHREDDED PARMESAN

4 THIN SLICES
4 BY 7-INCHES HAM,
ABOUT 4¼ OUNCES

SALT AND FRESHLY
GROUND BLACK PEPPER

BÉCHAMEL

4½ TABLESPOONS BUTTER

2 TABLESPOONS
ALL-PURPOSE FLOUR

4 CUPS MILK

NUTMEG, FOR GRATING

Serves 6

My neighbor Barbara makes this whenever asparagus is in season and we always love it when she brings us a piece. Use a dish measuring 9 by 13 inches as this will fit everything in. Barbara uses ready-to-bake lasagna sheets that don't need parboiling first. So easy.

Snap off the bottom third or so of the asparagus spears. You won't need these woody parts. Soak the top parts in a bowl of cold water for 10 minutes or so. Drain in a colander, then chop them up roughly. Heat the olive oil in a skillet and sauté the scallions until golden. Add the asparagus and water and cook until softened, then add the parsley. Season with salt and pepper. Put the lid on and cook for 10 minutes or so, until the asparagus are tender but not overcooked.

Preheat the oven to 350°C. To make the béchamel, melt the butter in a saucepan and then stir in the flour. Heat the milk in a separate pot and then slowly pour into the butter and flour, whisking to loosen it. When the milk is added and the mixture is smooth, simmer over low heat for 5 minutes or so to thicken slightly. Season with salt and pepper, and a grating of nutmeg. Remove from the heat and stir in the asparagus.

Start the assembly. Spoon a quarter of the béchamel over the bottom of the baking dish, spreading it to cover evenly. Cover with a layer (two sheets) of pasta, then one-third of the remaining béchamel, spreading it gently. Scatter 2 tablespoons of Parmesan over evenly. Tear two slices of ham in half and make a layer on top of the Parmesan. Add another layer of pasta, half the remaining béchamel, 2 tablespoons of Parmesan, then two slices of ham. Make a final layer of pasta, spread with the last of the béchamel, and scatter over the remaining Parmesan.

Bake for 20 minutes or so, until a bit crusty and golden here and there. Let cool a little before cutting into squares to serve.

PASTA AL FORNO
SICILIANA

4 TABLESPOONS OLIVE OIL

1 MEDIUM YELLOW
ONION, CHOPPED

2 MEDIUM CLOVES
GARLIC, CHOPPED

2 POUNDS 10 OUNCES
GROUND BEEF

½ TEASPOON
CHOPPED OREGANO

½ TEASPOON
CHOPPED THYME

1 BAY LEAF

1 CUP RED WINE

2 CUPS PUREED TOMATOES

7 OUNCES FROZEN PEAS

1 POUND RIGATONI PASTA

5½ OUNCES THINLY
SLICED HAM, TORN UP

9 OUNCES MOZZARELLA,
ROUGHLY CHOPPED

ABOUT 4 TABLESPOONS
SHREDDED PARMESAN, PLUS
EXTRA, FOR SERVING

SALT AND FRESHLY
GROUND BLACK PEPPER

Serves a neighborhood

This is what my Sicilian friends have for Sunday lunch. Traditionally, there are larger chunks of meat in the ragù, along with sausage and sometimes slices of boiled egg. It's normally followed by a crumbed meat or chicken cutlet and green salad. They say the lettuce is always there, one way or another. You'll need a 2½-inch-high, 9 by 13-inch baking dish.

Heat the oil in a deep skillet and sauté the ragù onion until golden. Add the garlic and sauté until it smells good, then add the ground beef. Brown the beef over quite a high heat, stirring often to break up any lumps. Stir in the oregano, thyme, and bay leaf, and season with salt and pepper. Stir in the wine and when that has been absorbed, add the tomatoes and 1 cup of water. Cover and simmer for an hour, stirring now and then. It must be a lovely loose *ragù*, so add a little water toward the end of cooking if necessary. Toss in the peas and remove from the heat.

Preheat the oven to 375°F.

Bring a large pot of salted water to a boil and cook the rigatoni to a couple of minutes short of the instructions on the package. Drain.

Scoop a couple of ladlefuls of the *ragù* onto the bottom of the baking dish. Add half the pasta, pressing it along to level it. Ladle on half the remaining *ragù* and top with all the ham. Scatter half the mozzarella on top, then follow with 2 tablespoons of Parmesan. Now add the rest of the pasta and press it down firmly. Scrape out the rest of the *ragù* over the top. Scatter the remaining mozzarella and Parmesan on top. Bake for 20 to 30 minutes, until it is a bit crusty on top here and there, and golden around the edges. Scoop out portions and serve with extra Parmesan.

PENNE WITH CALAMARI, ZUCCHINI & THEIR FLOWERS

Serves 4

Nice, summery, and so simple, especially if you have zucchini growing in abundance. It's also a good way of using some of those flowers that dress up the garden. Parmesan may not usually be served with this on account of the calamari, but I think it adds a lovely extra layer. You decide.

Clean the calamari. Remove the ink sac and the beaky part around the tentacles. Keep small tentacles whole and halve them if big. Pull out and discard the transparent quill and rinse the calamari well. Slice the body into rings and keep on a plate with the tentacles.

Rinse the zucchini flowers and remove the inner parts. Cut each flower into three or four chunks. Keep aside on paper towels. Meanwhile, heat 3 tablespoons of the olive oil in a large skillet and add the zucchini rounds and half the garlic. Season with some salt and sauté until the zucchini is cooked and golden in parts. Add the flowers and cook for just a moment. Scrape out into a bowl. Add the last 3 tablespoons of oil and the remaining garlic to the pan. When the garlic smells good, add the calamari and sauté for a minute or two. Season with the chili powder and salt and pepper. Add 2 tablespoon of the parsley and the wine and cook for a couple of minutes, until the wine reduces.

Meanwhile, bring a pot of salted water to a boil and cook the penne to al dente. Return the zucchini to the pan with the calamari and heat for a couple of minutes. Scoop out the pasta with a slotted spoon and mix with the calamari and zucchini, adding a little of the pasta cooking water to help it move smoothly along its way. Add the rest of the parsley, tossing the penne through gently and evenly. Serve in warm, wide pasta bowls, with a drizzle of olive oil, a good grind of pepper, and a little shredded Parmesan, if you wish.

SPAGHETTI WITH LENTIL RAGÙ

7 OUNCES SMALL
BROWN LENTILS

BUNCH OF FRESH SAGE

1 WHOLE MEDIUM CLOVE
GARLIC, PEELED

4 TABLESPOONS OLIVE OIL

1 MEDIUM RED ONION, CHOPPED

I (14-OUNCE) CAN
CHOPPED TOMATOES

GOOD PINCH OF CHILI POWDER

2 HEAPING TABLESPOONS
CHOPPED PARSLEY

14 OUNCES SPAGHETTI

FRESHLY SHREDDED PARMESAN,
TO SERVE, IF YOU LIKE

Serves 5

My friend Anjalika taught me this and it is wonderful. The kind of thing I want to make very often, served with a mixed green salad (see page 102). If you are making and serving the lentils right away, these liquid amounts are good. However, if you will be making the lentils ahead of time, they will absorb water as they sit, so you will need to add a little more water when heating through before serving. Sometimes I like to tear in a little fresh mint with the parsley.

Rinse the lentils, pick out and discard any hard odd bits, then put in a pot and cover with water. Add the sage and garlic and simmer, partly covered, for 25 minutes or so. Add a little hot water if the level becomes low and season with salt toward the end of the cooking time. Drain, keeping the cooking water.

Meanwhile, heat the olive oil in a saucepan and sauté the onion, stirring with a wooden spoon, until it is sticky. Add the tomatoes, a pinch of salt, pepper and the chili powder. Simmer, mashing down any large lumps, for 10 minutes or so, until the tomato has collapsed. Add the lentils, along with about 1 cup of the cooking water, and simmer, uncovered, for another 10 minutes, for all the flavors to combine. Add a drop more water, if it looks too thick or cook a little longer if too thin. Stir in the parsley and remove from the heat.

Meanwhile, cook the pasta in boiling salted water to al dente. Drain the pasta and serve in warm, wide pasta bowls. Ladle some lentil *ragù* over each (you may have some *ragù* left over—I like to serve it with boiled potatoes the next day). Some like this spaghetti with Parmesan, but others insist it should be served without.

RAGÙ WITH MILK &
GREEN TAGLIATELLE

5 TABLESPOONS
OLIVE OIL

1 MEDIUM RED ONION,
FINELY CHOPPED

1 CELERY STALK,
FINELY CHOPPED

1 CARROT, PEELED AND
FINELY CHOPPED

1 MEDIUM CLOVE CARLIC,
CHOPPED

1 POUND 2 OUNCES
GROUND BEEF

1 ITALIAN PORK SAUSAGE,
ABOUT 3½ OUNCES,
SKINNED AND CRUMBLED

NUTMEG, FOR GRATING

¾ CUP RED WINE

1²/₃ CUPS CANNED
CHOPPED TOMATOES

2 CUPS MILK

1 BATCH GREEN
TAGLIATELLE (PAGE 140)

FRESHLY SHREDDED PARMESAN,
TO SERVE

SALT AND FRESHLY
GROUND BLACK PEPPER

Serves 6 abundantly

This makes a good and richer-than-usual ragù, *on account of using milk instead of water. I love it. For some reason it is wonderful with green (spinach) tagliatelle. You can make this the day before if you want to break up the load—keep in the fridge and just heat through to serve the next day with your pasta.*

Heat the oil in a deep nonstick skillet and sauté the chopped vegetables until they are a bit golden. Add the garlic and sauté until it smells good, then add the ground beef and sausage and sauté until golden and sticky looking. Add salt and pepper, and an exceptionally good grating of nutmeg and stir well. Add the wine. Let it reduce to almost nothing and then add the tomatoes, letting the flavors meld for a few minutes.

Add the milk and bring back to a simmer. Cover with the lid, lower the heat, and simmer for about 1¼ hours, until it is lovely and thick and saucy. If it is too dry in the end, add a little milk and keep going.

Warm a large serving bowl. Bring a large pot of salted water to the boil. Add the pasta, dropping it in gently and distributing it evenly so it doesn't clump in a ball. From when it returns to the boil it should take 4 minutes or so to become tender, but taste to check. Scoop out the pasta with a spaghetti fork and toss gently with the hot sauce in the warmed serving bowl. Add a little of the pasta cooking water to help it along its way. Serve at once in warm, wide pasta bowls, scattered with shredded Parmesan.

GREEN TAGLIATELLE

8½ OUNCES YOUNG ENGLISH
SPINACH, TRIMMED
(6 OUNCES TRIMMED WEIGHT)

2 EGGS

2²/₃ CUPS ALL-PURPOSE FLOUR,
PLUS A TAD EXTRA, FOR ROLLING

1 TABLESPOON + 1
TEASPOON OLIVE OIL

Serves 6

This is easier than you might think—the most challenging part is taking the pasta machine out of the box and attaching it to the table. Once you have got over that block it is tremendously therapeutic. You will feel fabulous and may find yourself planning the next flavor of homemade pasta.

Wash the spinach well and drop in a pot of boiling salted water for a few minutes. Drain very well. When cool, squeeze out all the water you can, until your arms almost ache. Put it in a blender with 1 egg and pulse until pureed.

Pile the flour on your work surface. Make a well in the center and add the pureed spinach, the remaining egg, a pinch of salt, the olive oil, and 1 generous tablespoon of water. Use your hands to mix until combined, then knead until you have a soft, green dough. If it seems too dry, just pat your hands in water and continue. If too wet, pat your hands in flour. Put the ready dough in a bowl and cover with a cloth. Leave it to rest at room temperature for about half an hour or so.

Set up your pasta machine and have a little pile of flour next to you or on a board. Roll out about a quarter of the dough, keeping the rest covered with a kitchen towel so it doesn't dry out. Feed the rolled dough through the highest setting on the machine. Fold it up again like a book to neaten it and pass it through this setting again. Lower the setting to halfway on the machine and pass the dough through this setting twice, sprinkling a little flour onto the pasta to prevent sticking. Halve the dough now that it is longer, to make it more manageable. Lower the setting to the second-lowest one. Pass each sheet through twice to get two sheets of about 18 by 4¼ inches. Lay the sheets without touching on a lightly floured surface and leave them to dry for 15 minutes or so. Roll out the remaining portions of dough the same way.

Roll up a sheet of pasta loosely from one short end to the other. Without pressing, gently cut it into thin strips, about ½ inch wide, then unfurl them with your fingers. Have a couple of large trays lined with kitchen towels and scattered lightly with flour. Fluff the pasta out onto the trays with some of the flour so the strips won't stick together. Cut the remaining pasta sheets into strips. They can be cooked whenever you're ready.

SPAGHETTI WITH PANCETTA, PECORINO & ROSEMARY CRUMBS

THE LIST

8 TABLESPOONS OLIVE OIL

2 MEDIUM CLOVES GARLIC, PEELED AND SQUASHED WITH THE FLAT OF A KNIFE

⅔ CUP BREAD CRUMBS, MADE FROM DAY-OLD CRUSTLESS COUNTRY-STYLE BREAD

1 TABLESPOON CHOPPED ROSEMARY

1½ OUNCES PANCETTA, SLICED ABOUT 1/16 INCH THICK, ROUGHLY CUT UP

3 TOMATOES FROM A CAN

A LITTLE CHILI POWDER

12 OUNCES THICK SPAGHETTI OR PICI

1½ OUNCES THINLY SHAVED MATURE PECORINO OR PARMESAN

SALT AND FRESHLY GROUND BLACK PEPPER

Serves 4

This is my sister-in-law Luisa's recipe. The tomato here is not much—enough to give just a light coating. Use a day-old country-style bread for the crumbs.
The kind of pasta that Luisa would serve with this is pici, a thick, hand-rolled flour-and-water pasta that is much appreciated. A thick spaghetti would also be great.

To make the crumbs, drizzle 1 generous tablespoon of the olive oil here and there over the bottom of a large skillet that will eventually hold all your pasta. Add one clove of garlic and the bread crumbs and gently sauté until golden, stirring through with a wooden spoon so they all get a turn to tan evenly. Add the rosemary and a little salt (bread in Tuscany is generally unsalted, but if your bread is salted you may not need to add any). When the rosemary smells good and you have stirred it well and brought out its flavor, scrape the crumbs into a bowl. Wipe out the skillet with a paper towel and return it to the heat.

Put a pot of salted water on to boil for the pasta. In the skillet, heat the remaining 7 tablespoons of olive oil with the remaining clove of garlic and add the pancetta. Sauté until lightly golden, then add the tomatoes. Break them up with a wooden spoon and simmer for 5 minutes or so, just to warm them in the oil. Season with salt and chili powder.

Cook the pasta until al dente, scoop it out with a spaghetti fork and add to the sauce in the skillet. Add some of the pasta cooking water to help it along. Stir to distribute everything evenly, then divide among four warm, wide pasta bowls. Serve a little per bowl at first, as much of the good sauce goes to the bottom and it's not fair if the last portion gets it all. In fact, it is said that the guest should get the last plate. Pile the bread crumbs over the pasta, heap some shaved pecorino on top, and give a good grind of black pepper. Serve at once.

SAPIENTE

WORDS/PAROLE

TUTTI I NODI VENGONO AL PETTINE
(All the knots eventually come to the comb).

SPAGHETTI AGLIO, OLIO, PEPERONCINO & AVOCADO

4 TABLESPOONS OLIVE OIL

1 LARGE CLOVE
GARLIC, CHOPPED

1 SMALL DRIED
RED CHILE, CHOPPED

1 RIPE AVOCADO, NOT TOO BIG

JUICE OF ½ SMALL LEMON

5½ OUNCES SPAGHETTI

SHREDDED PARMESAN, TO SERVE

SALT AND FRESHLY
GROUND BLACK PEPPER

Serves 2

People are often surprised when I serve this twist on a traditional pasta. It is simple, yet rich and delicious. The avocado has to be a beauty, otherwise forget it. You should be generous with the salt and pepper to bring out its flavor.

Heat the oil and garlic over a very gentle heat in a small skillet to just draw out the flavor. Take care not to burn the garlic because you can ruin its flavor. When it smells good, add the chile and heat for a moment more. Remove from the heat. Halve the avocado and scoop out nice chunks into a wide serving bowl. Add the lemon juice and season well with salt and pepper.

Meanwhile, cook the pasta in boiling salted water until al dente. Pour the cooled garlic oil over the avocado and gently mix. Scoop out the pasta with a spaghetti fork directly into the bowl. Add a little of the cooking water to loosen things up and stir gently, trying to keep the avocado in chunks. Serve immediately with lots of shredded Parmesan and a nice extra grind of black pepper.

GIOVANNA'S SPAGHETTI

5 TABLESPOONS OLIVE OIL,
PLUS A LITTLE EXTRA, TO SERVE

1 CUP CHOPPED RED ONION

3½ OUNCES RED BELL PEPPER,
CUT INTO ½-INCH CHUNKS

6¼ OUNCES EGGPLANT, CUT
INTO ½-INCH CHUNKS

4 ANCHOVY FILLETS, CHOPPED

2 MEDIUM CLOVES
GARLIC, CHOPPED

1 CAN (14-OUNCE)
CHOPPED TOMATOES

2½ TABLESPOONS
CHOPPED PARSLEY

1½ HEAPING TABLESPOONS
EACH OF PITTED GREEN AND
BLACK OLIVES, CHOPPED
BIG OR JUST HALVED

PINCH OF CHILI POWDER

1 TABLESPOON SMALL CAPERS
IN VINEGAR, DRAINED

14 OUNCES SPAGHETTI

1 HEAPING TABLESPOON
MARJORAM LEAVES

FRESHLY SHREDDED
PARMESAN, TO SERVE

Serves 5

Giovanna is an incredible, tireless nonna *who just gives and gives. This is abundant, packed with goodies and full of flavor. The sauce goes well anytime, but particularly in summer when peppers and eggplants are at their best. Use basil instead of the marjoram, if you prefer.*

Heat the olive oil in a skillet that's large enough to hold your spaghetti later. Sauté the onion until softened and light golden. Add the pepper and eggplant and sauté until nicely cooked and a bit sticky. Add the anchovies and garlic, stirring briefly but well to make sure they simmer in the oil. When they smell good, add the tomatoes, parsley, olives, and a little salt (remember you have the olives and anchovies). Add the chili powder and a couple of grinds of pepper. Swish out the tomato can with a little water and pour it in. Cover and simmer for just under 10 minutes, until the sauce is loosely together but not too reduced. Add the capers when it is almost ready, then check the seasoning.

Cook the spaghetti in boiling salted water until al dente. Scoop out the pasta with a spaghetti fork directly into the pan of sauce, along with some of the cooking water so it's nice and loose but not too watered down. Tear up the marjoram leaves and toss well with the pasta. Divide among warm, wide pasta bowls. Serve hot with a small drizzle of olive oil, a scattering of Parmesan, and an extra grind of pepper.

SPAGHETTI WITH CLAMS, TOMATO & A DASH OF CREAM

1 POUND 2 OUNCES SMALL
CLAMS (VONGOLE VERACI)

2 MEDIUM CLOVES GARLIC,
PEELED, 1 LEFT WHOLE
AND 1 CHOPPED

4 TABLESPOONS OLIVE OIL

1 CUP CHOPPED TOMATOES

GOOD PINCH OF
CHILI POWDER

2½ TABLESPOONS HEAVY
WHIPPING CREAM

BUNCH OF PARSLEY
WITH STALKS

¼ CUP WHITE WINE

5½ OUNCES THICK SPAGHETTI

2½ TABLESPOONS
CHOPPED PARSLEY

SALT AND FRESHLY
GROUND BLACK PEPPER

Serves 2

Spaghetti with clams in one way or another is always popular. Here, tomatoes and just a little cream bring it together. The clams are cooked separately to the tomatoes in case they dislodge sand.

Soak the clams in a large bowl of cold salted water for a couple of hours to get rid of any sand. Give them a good swishing around in the soaking water a few times and change the water if there is any sand. Discard any clams that are well opened.

In a large skillet that will hold all the pasta later, stir the chopped garlic in 2 tablespoons of the olive oil until it smells good. Add the tomatoes and season with salt and pepper and the chili powder. Simmer for just under 10 minutes, squashing any tomato lumps with a wooden spoon. Add the cream and heat through, then remove from the heat.

In another pan that has a lid, heat the last 2 tablespoons of olive oil with the whole garlic clove. When the garlic has perfumed the oil, add the drained clams, parsley, and a grind of pepper. Pour in the wine. Put the lid on and turn the heat right up to steam the clams open. This should only take 5 minutes or so. Check to see if they've opened and give it a couple more minutes for any that haven't. Remove from the heat and let cool a tad. Discard any clams that haven't opened. When they are cool enough to handle, pluck out around half of the clam meat, putting it back in the pan and discarding those shells. Leave the rest of the clams in their shells in the pan. Remove the whole clove of garlic and parsley. Add the clams to the tomato pan, checking as you pour that there is no sand on the bottom of the pan and therefore giving no need to filter in the clam water.

Bring a pot of salted water to a boil and cook the spaghetti to al dente. When the pasta is just about ready, put the pan holding the clams over a high flame to heat through, then add the drained spaghetti. Stir well. Let it heat through for a minute, then scatter with the chopped parsley and serve at once with a good grind of black pepper. Serve with a plate for the shells.

SPAGHETTI WITH CLAMS & TABASCO

1 POUND 2 OUNCES SMALL
CLAMS (VONGOLE VERACI)

1 MEDIUM CLOVE
GARLIC, CHOPPED

2½ TABLESPOONS OLIVE OIL,
PLUS EXTRA, FOR SERVING

BUNCH OF PARSLEY
WITH STALKS

4 TABLESPOONS WHITE WINE

5½ OUNCES SPAGHETTI

½ TABLESPOON
CHOPPED PARSLEY

TABASCO SAUCE, TO SERVE

SALT AND FRESHLY
GROUND BLACK PEPPER

Serves 2

Here is a can't-get-simpler way with clams that has a good kick. Some people may like a squeeze of lemon juice over their serving. Follow this with a strongly flavored dish that won't pale by comparison.

Soak the clams in a large bowl of cold salted water for a couple of hours to get rid of any sand. Give them a good swishing around in the soaking water a few times and change the water if there is any sand. Discard any clams that are well opened.

In a large skillet that will hold all your pasta later, heat the garlic in the olive oil until it smells good. Add the drained clams, parsley, wine, and a grind of pepper. Cover and turn the heat right up to steam the clams open. This should only take 5 minutes or so. Check to see if they've opened and give it a couple more minutes for any that haven't. Remove from the heat and let cool a tad.

Discard any clams that haven't opened. When they are cool enough to handle, pluck out around half of the clam meat, putting it back in the pan and discarding those shells. Leave the rest of the clams in their shells in the pan. Remove the parsley. Check that there is no sand on the bottom of the pan and therefore no need to filter in the clam water.

Bring a pot of salted water to a boil and cook the spaghetti to al dente. When the pasta is just about ready, put the pan holding the clams over a high flame to heat through, then add the drained spaghetti. Stir well and let it heat together for a minute. Scatter with just enough parsley to add a dash of color and serve at once with a grind of black pepper and a good shake of Tabasco—as much as you can take. Serve with an extra drizzle of olive oil and a plate for the shells.

TORTA DI SPAGHETTI

THE
LIST

4¼ CUPS LEFTOVER COOKED
PASTA
(9 OUNCES UNCOOKED)

2½ TABLESPOONS OLIVE OIL

4 EGGS

5 TABLESPOONS SHREDDED
PARMESAN, PLUS A LITTLE
EXTRA, TO SERVE (OPTIONAL)

A FEW HERBS, CHOPPED

SALT

Serves 4

This is the thing to make when you have leftover pasta (okay, so you need a lot of it, but you never know). Or when you have an empty pan with some sauce clinging to it— scrape up all the clinging good stuff that was about to get rinsed out in the dishwater, it's such a potential building block. Of course, you can also make this from scratch, as I have often been asked to do by my children. Don't worry too much about precise amounts; it should just cover the bottom of the pan. You can get more elaborate and add mozzarellas and salamis, but that is another thing. Here is the basic route.

Have the cooked pasta at room temperature. Heat the oil in a 10½-inch nonstick pan and swizzle it around.

Add the pasta, flattening it like a neat nest. Whip the eggs in a bowl with a little salt. Pour out evenly over the pasta and stir to make sure all the pasta is coated. Flatten again. Panfry for a couple of minutes, then scatter the Parmesan and herbs evenly over the top. Cook for a couple of minutes more, until the egg is set and a bit crusty in places. Put on the lid and leave the pan off the heat for 5 minutes or longer, so the cheese melts a bit.

Loosen the edges with a wooden spatula, slipping it all the way underneath to make sure nothing is stuck. Have a large plate ready. Put the lid on the pan and flip the pan over so the *torta* is upside down on the lid. Now put the serving plate upside down over the *torta* and flip it back over with as much finesse as you can manage. Cut slices with a sharp knife and serve with a spatula. Serve hot with an extra scattering of Parmesan if you like.

BARBARA'S MOM'S
SPINACH POLPETTINE

1½ POUNDS YOUNG ENGLISH
SPINACH, TRIMMED
(1 POUND 2 OUNCES
TRIMMED WEIGHT)

9 OUNCES FRESH RICOTTA

NUTMEG, FOR GRATING

2½ TABLESPOONS
SHREDDED PARMESAN, PLUS
EXTRA, FOR SERVING

1 EGG, LIGHTLY WHIPPED

6 TABLESPOONS OLIVE OIL

1 MEDIUM CLOVE GARLIC,
PEELED AND SQUASHED
WITH THE FLAT OF A KNIFE

1 (14-OUNCE) CAN
CHOPPED TOMATOES

A FEW BASIL LEAVES, TORN

SALT AND FRESHLY
GROUND BLACK PEPPER

Serves 3 to 4

This recipe comes from Diana, my neighbor's mom. She is a great cook. It's very easy to make, with only a few ingredients, and it is healthy and always appreciated. Serve as a first course instead of pasta or rice.

Cook the spinach in boiling salted water for a few minutes. Drain it very well, pressing out the water. Let cool, then chop it up finely and put in a bowl. Add the ricotta, a good grating of nutmeg, the Parmesan, and egg, mixing it all well together. Taste for salt and pepper.

Preheat the oven to 350°F.

Heat 3 tablespoons of the olive oil in a saucepan with the squashed garlic. Add the tomatoes and basil and season with salt and a little pepper. Swirl about ½ cup of water around in the tomato can and add that, too. Simmer for 5 minutes or so. If there are still big bits of tomato, crush them with a fork or potato masher. Remove from the heat.

Drizzle the remaining 3 tablespoons of olive oil into an oval baking dish, roughly 10½ by 5½ inches. Spoon about one-third of the tomato sauce over the bottom of the dish. Take a tablespoon of the spinach mixture and edge it off gently with another spoon onto the tomato sauce in the dish. Continue with the remaining spinach mixture, resting the balls in compact rows. You will have about sixteen balls. Dollop the rest of the tomato sauce over the balls. It's best if most of them are covered, at least in part.

Bake for 20 to 25 minutes, until a bit golden here and there. Serve warm, scattered with Parmesan.

RISOTTO WITH SHRIMP, LAVENDER & LEMON

◇◇

This is delicate, summery, and delicious. You may like to add a shower of fresh herbs at the end. Have the butter and cream at room temperature.

Shell and devein the shrimp, discarding the heads and reserving the shells. Make the vegetable broth, adding the shrimp shells to the pot with the vegetables. Keep hot.

Heat half of the butter in a large, wide pot and sauté the scallions gently until cooked and pale golden, but not too dark. Add the rice and cook until it starts to stick, stirring it with a wooden spoon. Pour in the wine and cook until it has mostly vanished. Add 2 cups of the hot broth and simmer, stirring now and then with a wooden spoon, until the liquid has been absorbed by the rice. Add another 1 cup of broth and 2 to 4 of the lavender sprigs. Depending on your broth, you may need to add salt and pepper here. Once this broth has been gently absorbed, continue to add more broth, letting it simmer and absorb before adding the next cupful. The risotto is ready when the rice is creamy yet still a little firm, and there is just a small amount of liquid in the pot, about 20 minutes. If you run out of broth, you can use hot water.

Meanwhile, put a nonstick skillet over high heat with half the remaining butter and when it's hot, add the shrimp. Sauté until they are opaque and a bit golden on both sides. Add 1 teaspoon of the lemon zest with a little salt and pepper and toss together. Add the brandy and stand well back as if it flames up, it can be very exaggerated. Let it evaporate, then turn off the heat.

Add the cream and the last of the butter to the risotto. Stir to finish, or *mantecare*, as they say in Italy. Scrape in the shrimp and the other teaspoon of lemon zest and heat through just for a couple of minutes to amalgamate all the flavors. Taste and adjust the seasoning. Add extra hot water or broth if the risotto is too thick. Remove the lavender and serve at once, with some fresh lavender sprigs on top. Give a good grind of black pepper and scatter with Parmesan, if you wish.

1½ POUNDS MEDIUM RAW SHRIMP

5 CUPS QUICK VEGETABLE BROTH (PAGE 156)

7 TABLESPOONS BUTTER

¾ CUP CHOPPED SCALLIONS WITH SOME GREEN

1½ CUPS ARBORIO OR CARNAROLI RICE

¼ CUP WHITE WINE

ABOUT 12 FRESH UNSPRAYED LAVENDER SPRIGS

2 TEASPOONS FINELY GRATED LEMON ZEST, YELLOW PART ONLY

5 TABLESPOONS BRANDY

5 TABLESPOONS HEAVY WHIPPING CREAM

SHREDDED PARMESAN, TO SERVE, IF YOU LIKE

SALT AND FRESHLY GROUND BLACK PEPPER

Serves 4

RISOTTO WITH PEARS & PECORINO

5 TABLESPOONS OLIVE OIL

1 SPRING ONION, CHOPPED

1½ CUPS ARBORIO OR
CARNAROLI RICE

½ CUP WHITE WINE

2 LOVELY RIPE PEARS (ABOUT
12 OUNCES TOTAL)

5 CUPS QUICK VEGETABLE
BROTH (SEE BELOW), HOT

2¾ OUNCES FRESH PECORINO,
CHOPPED INTO CUBES

1½ OUNCES SHREDDED
MATURE PECORINO

2¾ OUNCES OR SO SHAVED
MATURE PECORINO

GROUND CINNAMON, TO SERVE

SALT AND FRESHLY
GROUND BLACK PEPPER

Serves 4

I use two types of pecorino here—a fresher one to turn through the risotto and melt a bit, and a good firmer, mature one for shredding in and shaving on top. You can use Parmesan if you can't find a mature pecorino. I love this with a dusting of cinnamon, as I ate it in a restaurant— try it with and without to see which way you prefer.

Heat the olive oil in a large, wide pot and sauté the spring onion until pale golden and softened. Add the rice and cook for a couple of minutes, stirring. Next, add the wine and let it sizzle and evaporate. Peel, core, and chop one of the pears into cubes, then add to the pan. Stir to blend the flavors, then add about 2 cups of the broth. When that has been absorbed, add another cup or so of broth. Depending on your broth, you may need to add salt and pepper here. When this broth has been gently absorbed continue to add more, letting it simmer and absorb before adding the next cupful. The risotto is ready when the rice is creamy yet still a little firm, and there is just a small amount of liquid in the pot, about 20 minutes. If you run out of broth, you can use hot water.

Peel, core, and chop up the second pear and add it to the risotto along with the fresh pecorino. Stir to meld the flavors, then stir in the grated mature pecorino. Serve immediately, dividing the shaved pecorino over the top, then adding a dusting of cinnamon for whoever wants it and a generous grind of black pepper over each.

QUICK VEGETABLE BROTH

1 CARROT

1 SMALL YELLOW ONION, PEELED

1 CELERY STALK

1 WHOLE MEDIUM CLOVE
GARLIC, PEELED

A FEW PEPPERCORNS

HANDFUL OF FRESH HERBS

SALT

Makes about 1 1/3 quarts

Put 7 cups of water, the carrot, onion, celery, garlic, and peppercorns in a pot with some salt and bring to a boil. Skim the surface if necessary, then simmer for about 30 minutes. Add the herbs to infuse for the last 5 minutes or so. Strain to use.

— THE —

Dining Room

— POULTRY & RABBIT —

CHICKEN WITH PEPPERS

RABBIT, PANCETTA & ROSEMARY PÂTÉ

MARISA'S ROAST CHICKEN

BAKED CRUMBED CHICKEN WITH MOZZARELLA,
ANCHOVIES & CAPERS

CHICKEN BREAST PIE WITH PORCINI & SAGE

CHICKEN WITH SALSICCIA & FENNEL

BROILED GALLETTI

CHICKEN CIABATTA WITH VALERIANA,
PECORINO & HAZELNUT SALAD

COLLO RIPIENO

ROAST LEMON & THYME CHICKEN

ROAST RABBIT WITH GRAPES

STUFFED GUINEA FOWL

SAPIENTE

WORDS/PAROLE

DRINK A MIXTURE OF
1 TEASPOON VINEGAR AND
1 TEASPOON SUGAR TO
STOP HICCUPS.

CHICKEN
WITH PEPPERS

If you love peppers, you will love this. It looks as if it almost cooked itself and came right to your table. It is perfect in summer when peppers are ripe and at their best. You can just pile all the ingredients in, put it in the oven, and then lie down and read a book. There is nothing else to do.

Preheat the oven to 350°F. Halve the peppers, remove the seeds, and chop each half into about four rustic pieces. Put in a 9 by 13-inch casserole dish and add the chicken, garlic, bay leaves, rosemary, olives, and olive oil. Season with salt and pepper and mix it all through with your hands. If it really is too thick to stir, mix in a large bowl and return to the dish. Cover with the lid. Put in the oven and bake for about 1½ hours, or until the chicken is cooked through and soft and the peppers are gorgeous.

Take off the lid and bake for another 20 minutes or so to give some blush to the chicken. Serve warm, with bread. Bread here is essential. If the skin of the peppers is starting to come away and it bothers you, just slip it to the side of the plate.

RABBIT, PANCETTA & ROSEMARY PÂTÉ

1 RABBIT (ABOUT 2½ POUNDS),
CUT UP INTO 8 TO 10 PIECES

14 OUNCES SLICED
ROUND PANCETTA

1 MEDIUM YELLOW
ONION, PEELED

2 WHOLE MEDIUM CLOVES
GARLIC, PEELED

1½ HEAPING TABLESPOON
CHOPPED ROSEMARY

1½ TEASPOONS FINE SALT

5 TO 6 BLACK PEPPERCORNS

Serves many

This recipe comes from Lydia's friend. She always makes a double dose and takes one to a friend. You could use a pressure cooker to shorten the cooking time. If so, add just enough liquid to cover. Serve this with broiled bread.

Rinse the rabbit under cold water and remove any fat and unwanted bits. Put in a pot with the water. Roll up the pancetta slices a few at a time and cut with kitchen scissors into the pot. Add the onion, garlic, rosemary, salt, and peppercorns. Bring to a boil. Cover and simmer until the rabbit is very tender, about 1 hour 15 minutes. Remove the rabbit pieces (reserving the liquid) and let cool a little, but they should still be a bit warm when you clean and puree them.

Remove the meat from the rabbit bones. Squelch the meat through your fingers (this is rather therapeutic) into a bowl to make sure no small bits of bone remain. Be thorough. Put the pancetta, onion, and cleaned rabbit meat in the bowl of a food processor and add about ¾ cup of the cooking water. Pulse to blend the mixture to a smooth puree. Taste for seasoning.

Line a 12 by 4¼ by 2½-inch loaf pan with a double thickness of waxed paper. Leave some overhang on the long sides. Scrape in the rabbit puree and smooth the surface. Fold the overhanging waxed paper across to cover the top, then put the tin in the fridge overnight.

To serve, lift the pâté from the pan, using the overhanging paper, and turn upside down onto a plate. Top with a few good grinds of pepper. Serve at room temperature with broiled bread and a nice salad.

SAPIENTE

WORDS/PAROLE

MEGLIO UN UOVO OGGI
CHE UNA GALLINA DOMANI
*(Better an egg today than
a hen tomorrow).*

MARISA'S ROAST CHICKEN

THE

LIST

1 CHICKEN (ABOUT 3
POUNDS 2 OUNCES)

2½ TABLESPOONS OLIVE OIL

2 TABLESPOONS ROSEMARY
& SAGE SALT (PAGE 24)

Serves 4

This is plain, rustic, simple, and healthy on account of having hardly any oil. It is nice with olive mash (see page 239) or a potato salad.

Preheat the oven to 400°F. Rinse the chicken and pat dry with paper towels. Flick a little water onto the bottom of a roasting dish and cover with a piece of baking parchment. Drizzle the oil over the chicken, add the herbed salt, and rub all over the skin. Put in the roasting dish, breast up, and roast for about 30 minutes. Baste, then pour off the excess liquid from the bottom of the dish and return the chicken to the oven, basting a couple of times more, for a further 40 minutes, or until it is cooked through, crusty, and golden. Cut the chicken into pieces so it's quick and easy to serve.

BAKED CRUMBED CHICKEN WITH MOZZARELLA, ANCHOVIES & CAPERS

4 SINGLE SKINLESS BONELESS
CHICKEN BREASTS, TRIMMED
OF ANY FAT AND BITS OF BONE

4 TABLESPOONS
CHOPPED PARSLEY

1 TEASPOON CHOPPED THYME

1 MEDIUM CLOVE
GARLIC, CHOPPED

4 ANCHOVY FILLETS, DRAINED,
CHOPPED BUT NOT TOO FINE

1 TEASPOON CAPERS IN
VINEGAR, DRAINED, CHOPPED

3½ OUNCES MOZZARELLA,
CUT INTO SMALL DICE

2 LARGE SLICES
DAY-OLD CRUSTLESS
COUNTRY-STYLE BREAD

1½ HEAPING TABLESPOON
GRATED PARMESAN

1 EGG

5 TABLESPOONS OLIVE OIL

1½ TABLESPOONS BUTTER

SALT AND FRESHLY
GROUND BLACK PEPPER

Serves 4

These buttery crumbed chicken breasts, stuffed with mozzarella, anchovies, and herbs, go well served with a gentle pile of mashed potatoes. The thin strip on the underside of the chicken breast that cuts away naturally (tenderloin) is not needed here. Use it in a soup or risotto, or to make mini fried chicken schnitzels for small panini.

Preheat the oven to 350°F. Wipe the chicken breasts clean with paper towels. Cut a long, deep pocket in each one through the thickest side, being careful not to cut all the way through or the filling will ooze out. Scatter a little salt and pepper over both sides of the chicken. Mix 2 tablespoons of the parsley with the thyme, garlic, anchovies, capers, and mozzarella in a small bowl. Divide among the chicken breasts and stuff well into the pockets. Use two toothpicks to seal off each opening.

Pulse the bread in a food processor to give uniform soft crumbs. Transfer to a plate and mix in the remaining 2 the egg in a wide bowl with some salt and black pepper. Dip the chicken breasts in the egg and then pat gently into the crumbs, helping them stick with your hands.

Put 2½ tablespoons of the oil and the butter in a baking dish just large enough to hold the chicken snugly. Add the chicken, drizzle with the remaining 2½ tablespoons of oil, and bake for 30 minutes or longer, until deep golden and slightly crispy. Remove from the oven and let rest, covered with foil, for 5 minutes or so. Remove the toothpicks and slice each breast on the diagonal into about six slices. Put on serving plates, drizzle each with a little juice from the pan, and give a final grind of black pepper. Serve with a squeeze of lemon juice if you like.

CHICKEN BREAST PIE
WITH PORCINI & SAGE

THE
LIST

2 SINGLE SKINLESS, BONELESS
CHICKEN BREASTS, TRIMMED
OF ANY FAT AND BITS OF BONE

2½ TABLESPOONS OLIVE OIL

4 LARGE THYME SPRIGS

4 LARGE SAGE LEAVES

1 ROSEMARY SPRIG,
NOT TOO LARGE

2¾ OUNCES MASCARPONE

9 OUNCES POLISH PUFF PASTRY
(PAGE 51)

1 EGG, LIGHTLY BEATEN,
FOR BRUSHING

7 OUNCES FRESH PORCINI
MUSHROOMS (SEE
GLOSSARY, PAGE 329)

4 TABLESPOONS OLIVE OIL

1 MEDIUM CLOVE GARLIC,
PEELED AND SQUASHED
WITH THE FLAT OF A KNIFE

6 TO 8 SAGE LEAVES

Serves 2 to 3

I love savory food wrapped in pastry. These chicken breasts are coated in herbs and mascarpone before being wrapped in pastry and baked. If you don't want to make your own puff pastry, just use a bought one. You can use any fresh mushrooms if you can't get fresh porcini.

Salt and pepper the chicken breasts well on all sides. Heat the oil in a nonstick skillet, and when hot, add the chicken. Cook until nicely golden on all sides. They will finish cooking in the oven but they must have a good crust. Transfer to a plate to cool.

Preheat the oven to 400°F. Strip the herbs off their stems and chop them up together. You'll need a generous 2 tablespoons. Mix into the mascarpone with a little salt. Cut the pastry in half and roll each out into a rectangle large enough to wrap a chicken breast.

Spread one-quarter of the mascarpone mixture onto the middle of each rectangle in a square that the chicken will sit on. Put the chicken on top and spread with the remaining mascarpone. Carefully wrap up the pastry in a good parcel around the chicken, not too tightly or the chicken might burst out, and making sure that it is generous at the seam. Put the parcels on a baking sheet lined with waxed paper. Brush the top of each with egg and bake for about 25 minutes, or longer if necessary, until the pastry is puffed, golden, and glossy. Remove from the oven and let rest for 10 to 15 minutes before serving.

Meanwhile, cut off the porcini stems and slice thickly, along with the caps. Heat the olive oil in a large nonstick skillet over high heat and add the garlic and porcini stems. Sauté until the garlic smells good, then add the caps. Continue cooking, and when the porcini brown a little, add the sage. Cook, stirring, until the sage is crisp.

Serve whole or in ½-to ¾-inch slices, with the hot porcini on the side.

CHICKEN WITH SALSICCIA & FENNEL

THE LIST

1 CHICKEN (ABOUT 2 POUNDS 10 OUNCES) SKIN REMOVED AND CUT INTO 8 PIECES

2 FENNEL BULBS (ABOUT 7 OUNCES EACH)

4 TABLESPOONS OLIVE OIL

1 MEDIUM WHITE ONION, CHOPPED

1 CELERY STALK, CHOPPED

1 LARGE CLOVE GARLIC, CHOPPED

3 ITALIAN PORK SAUSAGES (ABOUT 3½ OUNCES EACH), SKINNED (SEE GLOSSARY, PAGE 329)

½ CUP WHITE WINE

1 TEASPOON FENNEL SEEDS, CRUSHED

ABOUT 2 CUPS HOT WATER

SALT AND FRESHLY GROUND BLACK PEPPER

Serves 4

This dish is lovely with potatoes, either mashed or boiled, cooked greens, and bread for the juice.

Rinse the chicken and pat dry with paper towels. Rinse and trim the fennel, keeping the fronds. Cut the fennel lengthwise into quarters, keeping the quarters joined at the bottom. Heat the oil in a large skillet and sauté the onion and celery until golden. Add the garlic and cook until it smells good, then crumble the sausages into the pan. Cook until they have taken on a good color. Add the chicken and sauté until golden in parts.

Add the wine and let it evaporate, then add the fennel quarters, crushed fennel seeds, and salt and pepper. Pour in the water, cover with the lid, and simmer for 45 minutes to an hour. Take off the lid for the last 10 minutes to reduce any thin sauce—the end result must be saucy, but not too liquidy. Remove from the heat. Tear in a few fennel fronds here and there. Serve with bread.

SAPIENTE

WORDS/PAROLE

DON'T KINDLE A FIRE THAT
YOU CAN'T PUT OUT.

BROILED GALLETTI

2 GALLETTI
(BABY CHICKENS/POUSSINS,
ABOUT 1 POUND EACH)

JUICE OF 1 LEMON

5 TABLESPOONS OLIVE OIL

½ DRIED RED CHILE WITH
SEEDS, CHOPPED

1 TEASPOON OR SO
TABASCO SAUCE

1 HEAPING TABLESPOON
CHOPPED ROSEMARY

1 FRESH BAY LEAF,
TORN IN HALF

2 MEDIUM CLOVES GARLIC,
PEELED AND SQUASHED
WITH THE FLAT OF A KNIFE

SALT AND FRESHLY
GROUND BLACK PEPPER

Serves 2 generously

These are tender, marinated poussins that are cooked under the oven broil. Not too chile or herby, but delicate and just the right flavor. You can cook them on a barbecue if you like.

Cut the *galletti* down the backbone and open out to flatten. Rinse and pat dry with paper towels. Salt and pepper both sides, then lay them in an oven dish large enough to take them side by side.

Mix the lemon juice, olive oil, chile, Tabasco sauce, and rosemary together in a bowl and pour over the galletti. Tuck the bay leaf and garlic in between. Massage the flavorings into the *galletti* well, making sure all sides are covered. Leave them skin side up. Cover the dish with plastic wrap and put in the fridge for at least an hour, but as long as overnight.

Preheat the broiler. Turn the *galletti* skin side down. When the broil is hot, put the oven dish under and broil the *galletti* for about 45 minutes, turning them after 25 minutes, or when brown on the top. Continue broiling, skin side up now, until the skin is crisp and golden. Toward the end of broiling you may need to add a little water to the dish to prevent the sauce from drying out too much. Remove from the broiler and let rest for 10 minutes before serving. Serve with a salad with fresh blossoms.

CHICKEN CIABATTA
WITH VALERIANA,
PECORINO & HAZELNUT SALAD

Serves 3

I love fried chicken, especially in a ciabatta panino with lots of lemon squeezed in for some moisture and taste, and some salad leaves. This is a little more elaborate. It is lovely when the chicken is warm, but if you need to fry the chicken ahead of time it is also good cold.

Prepare the salad on the plates but don't dress it just yet.

Slice the chicken breast horizontally into three portions. They don't have to be exactly the same size; just go with the natural curves where you need to. Pound each one out a little with a meat mallet. Whisk the egg in a bowl with the thyme and a little salt and pepper. Pour into a wide bowl. Put the chicken in the egg and turn to coat all over. (This step can be done in advance—keep in the fridge, covered, until required.)

Mix the bread crumbs and Parmesan together on a flat plate. Lift each piece of chicken from the egg and pat each side firmly into the crumbs. Put the crumbed chicken on a plate. Heat enough oil to cover the bottom of a large skillet, and when it's hot, add the chicken. Panfry until firm and deep golden on the underside, then turn and cook the other side. Transfer to a plate lined with paper towels and keep them warm.

Halve each piece of ciabatta horizontally and fill with the chicken. Now dress the salad and serve it inside the panino or alongside. Squeeze some lemon juice on if you like. Close the panino, squash it so the juices go onto the bread, and eat right away.

VALERIANA, PECORINO & HAZELNUT SALAD

½ OUNCE SKINNED HAZELNUTS,
ROUGHLY CHOPPED

2¾ OUNCES MATURE PECORINO

1½ OUNCES SCALLIONS,
TRIMMED

1¾ OUNCES VALERIANA
(LAMB'S LETTUCE; SEE
GLOSSARY, PAGE 329)
OR WATERCRESS

3 TO 4 TABLESPOONS OLIVE OIL

JUICE OF ABOUT ½ LEMON

Serves 3

This is my friend Lisa's addition to our chicken ciabatta. She likes to layer her salad in this way. I love the details of keeping the white and green onion rings separate, and separating the individual rings. So much gentler in the mouth.

Toast the hazelnuts lightly in a dry skillet, taking care not to take them too far as this will make them bitter. Keep aside. Shave the pecorino thinly on the slotted side of a cheese grater, or with a potato peeler if you prefer. It looks good when the shavings are not uniform. Thinly slice the scallions, keeping the white and green parts separate.

Divide the *valeriana* among three serving plates. Scatter the white onion rings over, separating them out into individual rings. Drizzle each salad with about 3 teaspoons of olive oil and squeeze a little lemon juice over each. Add generous grinds of salt and black pepper. Top with shavings of pecorino, then the green part of the scallions, and finally, garnish with the hazelnuts. Gently toss the salad on the plate before eating.

SAPIENTE

WORDS/PAROLE

WASTE NOT
WANT NOT

**2 CHICKEN NECKS WITH
HEADS ATTACHED**

1 MEDIUM CARROT

1 CELERY STALK

1 MEDIUM YELLOW ONION

STUFFING

4½ OUNCES GROUND BEEF

**1½ OUNCES ITALIAN PORK
SAUSAGE, PROSCIUTTO OR
MORTADELLA, CHOPPED**

**5½ OUNCES CHICKEN LIVERS,
TRIMMED AND CHOPPED**

**2¾ OUNCES CRUSTLESS
DAY-OLD BREAD, SOAKED
IN MILK FOR 30 MINUTES
AND SQUEEZED DRY**

**1½ OUNCES SHREDDED
PARMESAN**

2 EGGS

GOOD GRATING OF NUTMEG

**GRATED ZEST OF 1 LEMON,
YELLOW PART ONLY**

Serves 2

COLLO RIPIENO

*This is a very authentic Tuscan housewives' recipe, with
the mentality of not wasting anything. You might like to try it
if you get your chickens whole. It has a rather old-fashioned
feeling. Wilma recommends serving it with Salsa Verde
(see page 18) and Preserved Vegetables (see page 14).
Cut off the chicken necks so they're as long as possible.*

Wash the chicken necks, then slide the inner bones out
of each one. Tie off the heads at the end of the necks
to ensure the stuffing stays in the necks. Mix everything
for the stuffing together well. Stuff the necks, but don't
exaggerate the amount or they could tear during cooking.
Sew the open ends closed so nothing will leak out.

Put a pot of salted water on to boil with the carrot,
celery, and onion. Add the chicken necks and simmer for
about an hour, checking that they stay covered with water
throughout. Use a pin to prick the necks to see if they are
ready—they are done when no liquid seeps out. Remove
from the liquid and let cool, so they are easier to slice.

ROAST LEMON
& THYME CHICKEN

1½ LEMONS

1 WHOLE CHICKEN (ABOUT
3 POUNDS 2 OUNCES)

2 MEDIUM CLOVES GARLIC,
ROUGHLY CHOPPED

4 TABLESPOONS OLIVE OIL

2 SMALL FRESH BAY LEAVES

HANDFUL OF THYME SPRIGS

2½ TABLESPOONS HEAVY
WHIPPING CREAM

SALAD

2 LARGE HANDFULS OF
VALERIANA (LAMB'S LETTUCE;
SEE GLOSSARY, PAGE
329) OR WATERCRESS

2½ TABLESPOONS OLIVE OIL

1 TEASPOON DIJON MUSTARD

1 TABLESPOON RED
WINE VINEGAR

1 MEDIUM CLOVE GARLIC,
PEELED AND SQUASHED
WITH THE FLAT OF A KNIFE

———

Serves 4

Use a nonstick baking dish, one that will fit the chicken pieces snugly without the pan juices spreading thinly and burning. The dish I use is 8½ by 12 inches.

Cut eight slices, about ¼-inch thick, from the whole lemon. Cut the chicken into four pieces, following the natural curves of bone. Cut away the wing tips. Rinse the pieces and pat dry. Squeeze the lemon half and anything left from the whole lemon into your baking dish and add the chicken pieces, garlic, olive oil, bay leaves, and thyme. Add salt and pepper and turn the chicken pieces to coat them well. Leave, skin side up, for 1 hour or so to marinate.

Preheat the oven to 400°F. Tuck the lemon slices under the chicken with the garlic and thyme. It's good if they see some open air so they get caramelly golden, but not too much or they will burn and become bitter. If you see them burning during roasting, tuck them completely under the chicken. Roast for 30 minutes, then pour ½ cup of water around the edges. Roast for another 20 to 30 minutes, until the skin on top is lovely and crisp and the juices are deep golden and lovely. Add an extra drizzle of water in this time if needed.

While the chicken is roasting, prepare the salad. Rinse and dry the *valeriana* and put in a wide bowl ready for tossing later. Whip the oil, mustard, and vinegar in a small bowl, then add the garlic and season with salt and pepper. Leave to sit and mingle.

Take the dish from the oven. Remove the chicken and lemon slices to an oval platter and cut the chicken with poultry scissors into smaller pieces. Add the cream and ¼ cup of water to the dish and put on the stovetop to bubble up and reduce, scraping up any interesting bits caught on the base with a wooden spoon. When you are satisfied with the consistency turn off the heat. Stir the salad gently with about 2½ tablespoons of the dressing—it should be just a light coat, not a dressing gown. Taste and adjust the seasoning if necessary.

Divide among four serving plates. Add the chicken and drizzle the sauce on top. Serve with bread.

SAPIENTE
WORDS/PAROLE

BETTER TO KEEP THE OLD
BROOM THAT SWEEPS WELL
THAN TO GET A NEW ONE

ROAST RABBIT
WITH GRAPES

THE
LIST

1 RABBIT (ABOUT 2½ POUNDS)

6 TABLESPOONS OLIVE OIL

1 CUP WHITE WINE

ABOUT 20 JUNIPER
BERRIES, SQUASHED WITH
THE FLAT OF A KNIFE

2 MEDIUM CLOVES GARLIC,
PEELED AND SQUASHED
WITH THE FLAT OF A KNIFE

2 BAY LEAVES, TORN

4 THYME SPRIGS, PLUS EXTRA,
TO SERVE, IF YOU LIKE

3½ OUNCES PANCETTA,
CHOPPED

1 POUND 2 OUNCES BLACK
AND WHITE GRAPES

SALT AND FRESHLY
GROUND BLACK PEPPER

Serves 4 to 6

This is lovely to make in autumn when grapes are everywhere. I like to use black and white grapes—you might like to use seedless grapes if you can get them.

Cut up the rabbit into about twelve pieces and put in a good-sized bowl with 3 tablespoons of the olive oil, the wine, juniper berries, garlic, bay leaves, and thyme, and a few good grinds of black pepper. Leave, covered, for an hour or two to marinate, in the fridge if it is a warm day.

Heat the remaining 3 tablespoons of oil in a large deep pan. Lift the rabbit pieces from the marinade (reserve the marinade), shake out, then brown well on all sides. Add the pancetta and panfry that, too, until golden. Salt the rabbit pieces, then add the marinade to the pan along with 2 cups of water. Cover and simmer for 30 minutes. Add half the grapes, cover again, and simmer for 30 to 40 minutes or so. Add the rest of the grapes and simmer, uncovered, for 10 minutes more to slightly thicken the juices in the pan. Check the seasoning and serve.

STUFFED
GUINEA FOWL

1 GUINEA FOWL (ABOUT
3 POUNDS)

14 OUNCES GROUND BEEF

14 OUNCES ITALIAN PORK
SAUSAGE, SKINNED

1¾ OUNCES SHREDDED
PARMESAN

3 EGGS, LIGHTLY BEATEN

7 OUNCES YESTERDAY'S
CRUSTLESS BREAD, BATHED
IN MILK TO COVER

1½ TABLESPOON TRUFFLE
BUTTER (PAGE 19), SOFTENED

PINCH OF GRATED NUTMEG

5 TABLESPOONS OLIVE OIL

1 CUP WHITE WINE

SALT AND FRESHLY
GROUND BLACK PEPPER

Serves 6 to 8

This is my sister-in-law Luisa's wonderful recipe. She makes it for Christmas. Something like this is always elegant. I love to serve it with a variety of vegetables, especially cardoons.

Have your butcher debone the guinea fowl, keeping the skin intact. Keep the bones. You can do this yourself if you know how. Flame the skin side if it has any feathery bits still attached. Lay out a large double layer of foil on a work surface, shiny side down. Rub the surface with butter.

Preheat the oven to 350°F. To make the stuffing, put the ground beef, sausage, Parmesan, eggs and drained and squeezed-out bread in a bowl. Add the truffle butter, nutmeg, salt, and pepper. Work the ingredients well together to mix. Lay the guinea fowl skin side down on the foil and spread the filling over it, leaving the long sides free. Roll up compactly from one long side to the other. Salt and pepper the outside of the guinea fowl. Now fold the foil around it to seal completely.

Drizzle the olive oil over the bottom of an 9 by 13-inch baking dish, put the guinea fowl on top and layer the bones around. Bake for about 40 minutes, then add the wine and cook for about 30 minutes more. Remove the foil from the guinea fowl and return to the oven for about 15 minutes, until it looks golden and the juices are bubbling. Transfer the guinea fowl to a platter and keep warm. Discard the bones in the dish. Drizzle about 4 tablespoons of water into the dish and put on the stovetop to bubble up for a couple of minutes. Strain into a bowl. Cut the guinea fowl into ½-inch slices and serve with the hot pan juices.

— THE —

Dining Room

— MEAT —

FILLET WITH ROSE SALT

LAMB WITH PRUNES AND ROSEMARY
& SAGE SALT

ROSEMARY CRUMBED LAMB CHOPS,
AGRETTI & ARTICHOKE SALAD

ROAST LAMB & POTATOES WITH
WILD FENNEL & SUN-DRIED TOMATOES

MEATBALLS IN TOMATO

MEATBALLS FROM IL BOLLITO WITH POTATO

IL BOLLITO

STRACCIATELLA

IL LESSO RIFATTO WITH ONIONS

POLPETTONE WITH ONIONS

STUFFED ONIONS

SCALOPPINE WITH TOMATOES & CAPERS

PORK SHIN WITH APPLES

ARISTA WITH ROSEMARY & SAGE SALT

STOVETOP PORK IN BALSAMIC VINEGAR

PANCETTA DI MARISA

FILETTO IN CROSTA

IT IS SAID THAT A SCATTERING
OF ROSE PETALS CAN HELP
IN UNLOCKING EMOTIONS.

FILLET WITH ROSE SALT

2 (7-OUNCE) BONELESS BEEF
STEAKS, ABOUT ¾ INCH THICK

1½ TABLESPOON OLIVE OIL

ABOUT 2 TABLESPOONS BUTTER

2½ TABLESPOONS COGNAC

ROSE SALT (PAGE 24)

FRESHLY GROUND
BLACK PEPPER

Serves 2

This is subtle, elegant, and quite gorgeous. You can taste the texture of the salt and see the rose petals. You will need a heavy-bottomed skillet and a strong flame to give the steaks a good and golden crust. Serve with new potatoes boiled in their skins and then drizzled with olive oil and melted butter.

Bring the steaks to room temperature. Drizzle them with oil, then rub it into both sides. Heat the skillet over a high flame to very hot. Add the steaks and cook for 2 to 3 minutes, until crusty and golden underneath. Turn over and cook until golden underneath once more. Add the butter to the pan, shaking it a little to distribute. Standing well back from the pan, add the cognac. It will probably catch fire and then burn out, so take care. Scatter some rose salt over each steak, add a grind or two of black pepper, and remove from the heat. Let the steaks rest in the pan for 5 minutes in a warm place. Serve directly onto two warm plates, scraping the juices out on top and with an extra scattering of rose salt. Grind a little more pepper on if you like and serve immediately.

LAMB WITH PRUNES AND ROSEMARY & SAGE SALT

◇◇

THE
LIST

8 TABLESPOONS OLIVE OIL

1 LEG OF LAMB (ABOUT 3½ POUNDS), DEBONED

2½ TABLESPOONS ROSEMARY & SAGE SALT (PAGE 24)

12 PITTED PRUNES

2 MEDIUM CARROTS, PEELED AND CUT INTO LARGE CHUNKS

1 SMALL CELERY STALK

1 MEDIUM YELLOW ONION, PEELED AND HALVED

¾ CUP WHITE WINE

Serves 4 to 6

Beautiful, rich, and deep. Just delicious. I love this with Sautéed Artichokes & Potatoes (page 107) and some crusty bread. Ask your butcher to debone the lamb or do it yourself if you know how.

Preheat the oven to 350°F. Drizzle 5 tablespoons of the olive oil onto a baking pan of about 9 by 13 inches. Lay two large sheets of foil on a work top, shiny side down and overlapping to give a larger surface. Rub with butter to grease well.

Rinse the lamb and pat dry with paper towels. Trim off any exaggerated fat, but leave most of it on for flavor and moistness. Put the lamb on a cutting board, skin side down and opened up like a book. Mix together the remaining 3 tablespoons of oil and the herbed salt, and massage half of it over the inside of the lamb. Line up the prunes in pairs like soldiers, running lengthwise down the center of the lamb. Wrap the sides of the lamb over to enclose the prunes. Tie up with kitchen string in a few places to hold the shape while cooking.

Rub the rest of the herby oil mix all over the outside of the lamb, then place it in the center of the foil. Wrap up tightly, tucking in the sides. Put in the oiled pan and scatter the vegetables around (add the lamb bone, too, if you have it). Roast for about 40 minutes. Remove the foil from the lamb, scrape in any accumulated bits from the side of the pan, and splash in the wine. Return the lamb to the oven for another 40 minutes or so, turning the lamb once or twice to brown all the sides and spooning the juices over. Add a little extra water if needed. To test if the lamb is done, prick it with a fork. The juices should run out, but not be pink.

Transfer the lamb to a suitable dish. Cut away the string and leave it to rest for a bit while you make some gravy. Add ½ cup of water to the baking pan and put it on the stovetop to bubble up and thicken a little. Scrape down any interesting bits from the sides of the pan into the juices. Cut the meat into slices about ⅝ inch thick and serve hot, with the juices spooned over.

ROSEMARY CRUMBED LAMB CHOPS, AGRETTI & ARTICHOKE SALAD

THE LIST

6 NOT-TOO-THICK LAMB CHOPS

4 TABLESPOONS OLIVE OIL

2 MEDIUM CLOVES GARLIC, PEELED AND SQUASHED WITH THE FLAT OF A KNIFE

1 HEAPING TABLESPOON CHOPPED ROSEMARY

1 EGG, BEATEN

ABOUT 8 TABLESPOONS DRIED BREAD CRUMBS

LIGHT OLIVE OIL, FOR FRYING

SALT AND FRESHLY GROUND BLACK PEPPER

Serves 3

Agretti and Artichoke Salad (see page 202 for both) are refreshing partners for these fried lamb chops. Agretti (see Glossary, page 328), is available in spring. It is very beautiful and elegant, like dark green seaweedy spaghetti, and full of vitaminy goodness. Have your agretti *cooked and salad things ready to assemble so when you have fried the chops you can serve it all immediately.*

Rinse the lamb chops and pat dry with paper towels. On a board, pound the meat part with a meat mallet to flatten. Put the oil and garlic in a wide bowl with the rosemary, a sprinkling of salt and a few grinds of black pepper. Add the chops, turning them through to coat. Cover with plastic wrap and leave for an hour or so.

Put the egg in a wide bowl and the bread crumbs on a flat plate. Shake the lamb chops out of the marinade and dip in the egg, coating all sides. Remove from the egg and shake off the excess, then press each one firmly into the bread crumbs so they are coated on both sides. Finish breading all the lamb chops, keeping them on a plate until you are ready to fry them.

Heat enough light olive oil in a large skillet to cover the bottom. Add the chops and fry until golden and crusty underneath. Turn them over and check that you have enough oil in the pan or the crumbs will burn. Fry until golden underneath once more and cooked through. Transfer the lamb chops to a plate lined with paper towels to absorb any excess oil.

ABOUT 10½ OUNCES AGRETTI
(SEE GLOSSARY, PAGE 328)

2½ TABLESPOONS OLIVE OIL

1 GENEROUS TABLESPOON
FRESHLY SQUEEZED
LEMON JUICE

———

Serves 3

AGRETTI

Cut away the bottom stems of the *agretti*, leaving just the algae green parts on the top held together in clumps of two or three. You don't want individual strings. Rinse in a bowl of cold water and work through them, removing any unwanted things. You may feel as if you are combing a mermaid's knotty hair. Bring a pot of salted water to a boil, add the *agretti*, and boil for about 6 minutes, or until tender. Drain, then drizzle with the olive oil and lemon juice, and give a grind of pepper and extra salt if necessary. Mix through.

1 SMALL LEMON, HALVED

1 ARTICHOKE

2 FISTFULS (ABOUT
1½ OUNCES) VALERIANA
(LAMB'S LETTUCE; SEE
GLOSSARY, PAGE 329)
OR WATERCRESS

2 TABLESPOONS OLIVE OIL

VANILLA SALT (PAGE 25)

FRESLY GROUND BLACK PEPPER

———

Serves 3

ARTICHOKE
SALAD

Squeeze the juice from half the lemon into a bowl of water. Clean the artichoke, leaving a little of the stem. Cut away the top third or so of the bulb. Tear away as many leaves as necessary to get to the tender inner ones (you can nibble on the nibs of these). Halve it and scrape away the choke. Slice the halves into lengths of a couple of fractions of an inch each and drop these in the lemon water as you go so they don't go brown.

Put the *valeriana* in a bowl. Add the drained and patted-dry artichoke. Squeeze over the juice from the other lemon half and drizzle in the oil. Add a small scattering of vanilla salt, a few grinds of pepper, and gently turn through. Serve next to the lamb and *agretti*, with a few extra grains of vanilla salt over the artichokes if you like.

ROAST LAMB & POTATOES WITH WILD FENNEL & SUN-DRIED TOMATOES

1 SHOULDER OF LAMB (ABOUT 2 POUNDS 10 OUNCES), WITH ONLY THE HEAVY FAT REMOVED

4 TO 5 WILD FENNEL STALKS

6 TABLESPOONS OLIVE OIL

1 TEASPOON CRUSHED FENNEL SEEDS

3 MEDIUM CLOVES GARLIC, PEELED AND HALVED

5 TO 6 THIN ROSEMARY SPRIGS

5 TO 6 SAGE LEAVES

1 OUNCE PLUMP SUN-DRIED TOMATOES, THICKLY SLICED

1 CUP WHITE WINE

1 POUND 10 OUNCES POTATOES, SCRUBBED AND CUT INTO CHUNKS

SALT AND FRESHLY GROUND BLACK PEPPER

Serves 4

You will need a few long fresh wild fennel stalks to put in the bottom of the dish to perfume it all beautifully. I use a round dish, about 13½ inches in diameter, to cook this in. I like to serve it with a green salad (see page 102). If you can get crushed dried fennel flowers, use those instead of the fennel seeds here.

Preheat the oven to 400°F. Rinse the lamb and pat dry with paper towels. Cut five or six long slashes on the top. Make a bed of the fennel stalks on the bottom of a baking dish and drizzle 4 tablespoons of olive oil on top. Salt and pepper both sides of the lamb well and rub in the crushed fennel. Press a garlic half, a rosemary sprig, a sage leaf, and a few slices of tomato into each slash. Put the lamb on top of the fennel stalks and drizzle with the remaining 2 tablespoons of olive oil.

Roast until the top of the lamb is starting to change color, about 20 minutes. Pour in the wine and add the potatoes around the lamb, stirring them into the liquid. Lower the temperature to 350°F and roast for 1 hour 15 minutes, turning the potatoes a few times. The lamb should be golden, nicely cooked and soft, and the potatoes should be golden brown.

Serve the lamb cut in thick chunks, with the potatoes.

MEATBALLS
IN TOMATO

THE
LIST

10½ OUNCES GROUND BEEF

1 EGG, LIGHTLY BEATEN

1 HEAPING TABLESPOON
CHOPPED PARSLEY

1 HEAPING TABLESPOON
CHOPPED MINT

PINCH OF CHILI POWDER

2 MEDIUM CLOVES GARLIC,
PEELED, 1 CHOPPED AND
1 SQUASHED WITH THE
FLAT OF A KNIFE

2½ TABLESPOONS OLIVE OIL,
PLUS 4 TABLESPOONS
FOR PANFRYING

1 (14-OUNCE) CAN
CHOPPED TOMATOES

½ CUP RED WINE

4 BASIL LEAVES, TORN

SALT AND FRESHLY
GROUND BLACK PEPPER

Serves 2 to 3

These are lovely served with mashed potatoes, rice, or some crushed boiled potatoes.

In a bowl, mix the ground beef, egg, parsley, mint, chili powder and chopped garlic together and season with salt and pepper. Knead together well. Cover and put in the fridge for at least 30 minutes.

Heat 2½ tablespoons of the olive oil in a saucepan with the squashed clove garlic, and when it smells good add the tomatoes. Season with salt and pepper and simmer for about 10 minutes.

Shape the meat mixture into small balls the size of a walnut. Heat the other 4 tablespoons of olive oil in a large nonstick skillet, and when hot, add the meatballs and panfry gently until golden on all sides. Add the wine to the pan and let it reduce. Add the tomato sauce and the basil leaves, giving the pan a shake so it all mixes well. Cover and simmer for about 20 minutes. If it looks like it is drying out at any time, add a few drops of water. Taste for seasoning and serve warm.

MEATBALLS FROM IL BOLLITO WITH POTATO

¾ POUND POTATOES, WASHED

10½ OUNCES MEAT FROM
IL BOLLITO (PAGE 209)

1 MEDIUM CLOVE GARLIC,
FINELY CHOPPED

1 TABLESPOON
CHOPPED PARSLEY

1 EGG

2 TABLESPOONS
GRATED PARMESAN

NUTMEG, FOR GRATING

ABOUT 4 TABLESPOONS
DRIED BREAD CRUMBS

LIGHT OLIVE OIL,
FOR PANFRYING

SALT AND FRESHLY
GROUND BLACK PEPPER

Serves 4 to 6

Here is a wonderful way that Wilma uses meat from a bollito. Actually, you could use any cooked meat to make these. Wilma serves them with Stracciatella (page 209), made from the bollito broth.

Boil the potatoes in salted water until soft. Drain, and when cool enough to handle, peel and mash them. Chop up the meat finely, mix in the garlic, and mash into the potato. Add the parsley, egg, Parmesan, a good grating of nutmeg, and a grind of pepper. There should be enough salt from the potatoes and *bollito*, but check just in case.

Shape into patties about 2 inches or so in diameter and ½-inch thick. Put the bread crumbs on a plate, add the patties, and turn to coat all sides, pressing on the crumbs on with your fingers. Heat enough oil to cover the bottom of a nonstick skillet.

Panfry the patties, in batches if necessary, until golden all over, turning them carefully with a fork so they don't break. Transfer to a plate lined with paper towels to absorb excess oil. Give a small sprinkle of salt on top. These are good served with a squeeze of lemon juice or some herbed mayonnaise.

IL BOLLITO

THE
LIST

1 POUND 10 OUNCES FAIRLY LEAN
BEEF, IN ONE OR TWO PIECES

2 MEDIUM CARROTS

1 CELERY STALK

1 LARGE YELLOW ONION, PEELED

ABOUT 6 PEPPERCORNS

ABOUT 2 TEASPOONS SALT

Serves 4

This is the base for many dishes. The boiled meat can be served with various sauces and marmalades, or turned into other dishes. The brodo (broth) can be used in a soup or is delicious to simply drink from a cup (brodo in tazza). This one is a simple brodo. You can add anything you like, such as a bay leaf, potato, fresh thyme, or a whole tomato, depending on how you will be serving it. The meat needs a long time to cook and soften and you can make it in a pressure cooker if you prefer.

Rinse the meat and vegetables, then put in a pot. Cover with 8 cups of water and add the peppercorns and salt. Bring to a boil. Skim off the scum that rises to the surface, lower the heat, and put the lid on. Simmer for 2½ to 3 hours, until the meat is very tender when poked with a fork. Add extra water as it reduces. When it is ready, transfer the meat to a board and strain the broth.

STRACCIATELLA

THE
LIST

2 CUPS BRODO FROM IL
BOLLITO (SEE ABOVE)

1 EGG

GRATED PARMESAN, AT LEAST
2 HEAPING TABLESPOONS

Serves 2

A much-appreciated soup among all generations, made with a deep tasty broth. It is often served to the convalescing, the young, and the elderly. It needs that scattering of freshly grated Parmesan flung on top when it's hot and then you are left to slurp away at this in your pretence of being ill. Stracci are rags, and that's what the strands of egg in the broth look like.

Pour the *brodo* into a shallow saucepan. Heat to a good boil and check the seasonings. Adjust if necessary. Whip the egg in a small bowl with a whisk. Pour into the hot broth, whisking so it gets the long *stracci*. Remove from the heat at once and divide between two bowls. Scatter a heaping tablespoon, if not two, of Parmesan over each.

SAPIENTE
WORDS/PAROLE

SAME MEAT,
DIFFERENT GRAVY.

IL LESSO RIFATTO
WITH ONIONS

1 POUND 2 OUNCES MEAT
FROM IL BOLLITO (PAGE 209)

4 TABLESPOONS OLIVE OIL

2 LARGE RED ONIONS,
HALVED AND SLICED

1 MEDIUM CLOVE
GARLIC, CHOPPED

1 (14-OUNCE) CAN
CHOPPED TOMATOES

GOOD PINCH OF CHILI POWDER

½ TEASPOON DRIED OREGANO

1 HEAPING TABLESPOON
EACH OF PITTED GREEN
AND BLACK OLIVES

ABOUT 5 BASIL LEAVES, PLUS
A FEW EXTRA, TO SERVE

SALT AND FRESHLY
GROUND BLACK PEPPER

Serves 4

This rifatto (redone) style of cooking in Tuscany is common and takes very good care of leftovers. Here it is assumed you may have leftover bollito meat. If not, you can just start from scratch of course. I like to add olives to this dish.

Chop the meat into chunky slices. Heat the olive oil in a nonstick skillet and sauté the onions until softened, nicely golden and a bit sticky. Add the garlic and when it smells good stir in the tomatoes. Add the chili powder and oregano, and season with salt and pepper. Simmer for about 10 minutes. Add the meat and olives, and tear in the basil. Stir gently and cook until it is all harmonious, about 5 minutes. Serve with bread and a few torn basil leaves over the top.

CAFFE
WILMA

IL CAFFE GIUSTO

— AM —

CAFFÈ LATTE

*for the
morning
only*

— AM —

CAPPUCCINO

*only in the
morning*

— PM —

CAFFÈ CORRETTO

*for evening
or after lunch
or morning for
some*

— AM OR PM —

ESPRESSO

*acceptable
anytime*

— AM OR PM —

MACCHIATO

*acceptable
anytime*

POLPETTONE WITH ONIONS

2 OUNCES CRUSTLESS
COUNTRY-STYLE BREAD

¼ CUP MILK

2¼ POUNDS 4 OUNCES LEAN
BEEF, FINELY GROUND

3 EGGS, LIGHTLY BEATEN

3 TABLESPOONS
GRATED PARMESAN

A GOOD GRATING OF NUTMEG

2 TABLESPOONS
CHOPPED PARSLEY

4 TABLESPOONS OLIVE OIL

½ CUP WHITE WINE

1¼ POUNDS RED ONIONS, SLICED

SALT AND FRESHLY
GROUND BLACK PEPPER

Serves 6 to 8

This is Diana's recipe. She is a wonderful and elegant nonna and cook. She asks for the ground beef to be passed twice through the grinder as she likes it fine for this. Even though there are eggs, it's quite delicate and you have to take care while turning it in the pan so it doesn't break. If possible, use a large nonstick skillet with fairly high sides so that you can put a lid over the hill of meat in the pan. Lovely with a dish of sliced tomatoes on the side

Break up the bread, put in a bowl, and soak in the milk to soften. Put the meat in another bowl and add the eggs, Parmesan, nutmeg and parsley, and season with salt and pepper. Squeeze out the bread and add it to the bowl with the meat. Mix together, then knead very well. Put in the fridge for an hour or so.

Shape the mixture into a nice compact log that will just fit in your pan. Heat the oil in the pan and gently lower in the *polpettone*. Panfry until golden underneath, then very carefully roll to turn it, using a slotted spoon or similar in both hands. Fry until all the sides are golden and sealed, then lower the heat and simmer for half an hour or so. Add the wine, and when most of it has evaporated, add ½ cup of water. Cover and simmer until the meat is cooked through and clear juices seep out when you prick it and press with a skewer, another half hour or so. Carefully transfer the *polpettone* to a serving platter to rest, drizzled with some of the pan juices to keep it moist.

Add the onions to the juices remaining in the pan, along with a little salt and pepper. Sauté until the onions are golden, soft, and a bit sticky. Add ½ cup of water to loosen things up and continue to simmer. Keep hot. Cut the meat into slices about ⅝ inch thick, gently supporting them with your hand as you go so they don't collapse. Serve a couple of slices each, with a tablespoon or so of hot onions spooned on top.

STUFFED ONIONS

**6 LARGE RED ONIONS
(7 OUNCES EACH)**

7 TABLESPOONS OLIVE OIL

1¼ POUNDS GROUND BEEF

**4 HEAPING TABLESPOONS
CHOPPED PARSLEY**

**1 (14-OUNCE) CAN
CHOPPED TOMATOES**

JUICE OF 1 LEMON

Serves 6 to 8

Delicious. Delicious. My mother's recipe. These little onion rolls look beautifully roasted in their oven dish, all top to tail and back to back.

Bring a large pot of unsalted water to a boil. Using a small, sharp knife, carefully peel the skins off five of the onions, keeping them hinged at the bottom. Cut each onion with one slash lengthwise, but just halfway through to the other side. This is to help the leaves loosen away during boiling. Boil until tender, about 15 minutes. Drain and let cool a bit so you can handle them.

Peel and chop the remaining onion. Heat 3 tablespoons of the olive oil in a large nonstick skillet. Add the chopped onion and sauté until softened and a bit golden. Add the ground beef and stir through, cooking until all the liquid has evaporated and the beef is cooked and golden brown. Season with salt and pepper, and stir in the parsley. Stir in ½ cup of the tomatoes and cook for a couple of minutes. Remove from the heat.

Preheat the oven to 350°F. Have a large baking dish about 9 by 13 inches ready. Sit at a table. Gently remove the onion leaves from the stems, carefully unfurling them so they don't tear. You need each leaf opened out as far as possible. The outer ones will, of course, be larger. Put about a tablespoon of filling toward one end of a leaf and roll up neatly and tightly. Fill and roll all the leaves, no matter how small they are; just add less filling to the little ones. Sit them in the dish, all tightly next to each other like seals on a beach. You won't be able to fill and roll the very inner leaves, but sit these in the dish as well.

Mix the remaining tomatoes and 4 tablespoons of olive oil with the lemon juice in a bowl and season with salt and pepper. Pour this mixture over the onions and sprinkle a little salt over the onion tops sticking out above the sauce. Bake for about 1¼ hours, until roasty and the sauce is slightly thickened. Serve warm with bread. Even at room temperature, these are great.

SCALOPPINE WITH TOMATOES & CAPERS

THE LIST

1 EGG

8 THIN PIECES BEEF CARPACCIO, ABOUT 4 BY 3¼ INCHES EACH (6 OUNCES TOTAL)

ABOUT 6 TABLESPOONS DRIED BREAD CRUMBS

4 TABLESPOONS OLIVE OIL

1 MEDIUM CLOVE GARLIC, PEELED AND SQUASHED WITH THE FLAT OF A KNIFE

1 CUP CHOPPED TOMATOES (FROM A CAN)

3 OR 4 BASIL LEAVES

1 TABLESPOON CAPERS IN VINEGAR, DRAINED, CHOPPED QUITE FINE

SALT

Serves 4

I particularly love these very thin slices of meat, as they are buttery soft and just vanish in the mouth. Even though this takes a few minutes in the pan, you can make it a bit ahead of time. Leave in the pan, covered, then just warm up to serve, with a little water drizzled in to get it back to the right consistency.

Whip the egg in a wide bowl with a little salt and add the beef slices. Turn them over to coat. Put the bread crumbs on a plate. Remove the meat one slice at a time from the egg, shake off the excess, and pat both sides lightly in the crumbs to loosely coat.

Heat the oil in a large nonstick skillet and add the garlic and crumbed meat slices. Panfry quickly, until lightly golden underneath, then turn and fry the other side. Add the tomatoes to the pan, around and over the meat. Scatter a little salt over, tear in the basil, lower the heat, and simmer for 8 minutes or so. Add the capers for the last couple of minutes. Turn off the heat, cover, and leave for 5 minutes or so before serving. If not serving immediately, keep covered.

SAPIENTE

WORDS/PAROLE

A TAVOLA NON SI INVECCHIA.
(At the table one doesn't get old).

PORK SHIN
WITH APPLES

THE
LIST

2¼ POUNDS PORK SHIN

2 MEDIUM CLOVES GARLIC,
PEELED AND HALVED

8 SMALL SPRIGS ROSEMARY

4 TABLESPOONS OLIVE OIL

2 BAY LEAVES

¾ CUP WHITE WINE

2 (6 OUNCES EACH)
RED APPLES, UNPEELED

2½ TABLESPOONS BUTTER

3 SAGE LEAVES

4 JUNIPER BERRIES, SQUASHED

1 GENEROUS TABLESPOON
COGNAC

QUINCE JELLY
(PAGE 40), TO SERVE

SALT AND FRESHLY
GROUND BLACK PEPPER

Serves 2

Perfect with Quince Jelly (page 40) and Marisa's Potatoes with Crumbs (page 106).

Preheat the oven to 350°F. Rinse the pork shin and pat dry with paper towels. Make four deep incisions in the meat and put one garlic half and 2 sprigs of rosemary into each. Salt and pepper the outside of the pork well. Pour the olive oil over the bottom of a roasting pan, then add the pork and bay leaves. Roast until browned, about 40 minutes. Add the wine and roast for a further 1 hour 15 minutes, turning the pork a couple of times and adding a little water if necessary so it doesn't dry out.

Meanwhile, halve, core, and slice the apple halves. Melt the butter in a skillet and sauté the apple quickly with the sage, juniper, and a little salt and pepper. Keep the slices intact; don't overcook them. Standing well back from the pan, add the cognac and let it evaporate. Take care when adding it as it may flame up.

Transfer the pork to a board. Add ¼ cup of water to the roasting pan and let it bubble up on the stovetop to thicken. Carve slices of pork lengthwise along the shin and put on a serving plate. Pour the sauce on top and serve hot, with the apples and quince jelly on the side.

ARISTA WITH ROSEMARY & SAGE SALT

5 TABLESPOONS OLIVE OIL,
PLUS EXTRA, FOR SERVING

3 TABLESPOONS ROSEMARY
& SAGE SALT (PAGE 24)

ABOUT 2 POUNDS 10 OUNCES
BONELESS AND RINDLESS PORK
LOIN, BUT WITH SOME FAT

½ CUP WHITE WINE

Serves 6

I like to serve this with Marta's Mom's Fennel (page 103). Make sure you don't overcook the meat, it's nice when it is just slightly past the pink stage. Beyond this point it dries out easily. If you don't have any Rosemary & Sage Salt ready, you can make up a small amount now quickly. Leftovers are nice in panini the next day with some of the sauce and a little mustard.

Preheat the oven to 350°F. Combine 2½ tablespoons of the oil with the herbed salt. Put the pork on a board. Spike a hole from one end to the other, using the handle of a wooden spoon (not too thick), pushing it all the way through to create a tunnel. Use your fingers to stuff some of the herby oily mix in from both ends. Push it along with the handle of the wooden spoon to loosely fill the whole tunnel. This will give flavor inside and also look good when you slice the pork. Rub the rest of the herby oily mix all over the outside of the pork.

Lay a large sheet of foil on a work surface, shiny side down, and rub with butter. Put the pork in the middle and wrap up snugly. Drizzle the remaining 2½ tablespoons of oil over a baking pan of about 10 by 7 inches. Add the pork package and roast for about 30 minutes, by which time the juices around should be golden. Unwrap the pork, discard the foil, and pour the wine around.

Return the pork to the oven and roast for another 30 minutes or longer if necessary, until the pork is golden and the juices on the bottom of the dish are gooey. If the juices look as if they are drying up during that time, drizzle a little water into the pan. Pour in about ½ cup of water 10 minutes before the end of cooking. The pork is done when you press it with a fork and the juices run out clear, not pink. Rest it in the pan for 10 minutes or so, then transfer to a board. Serve in thin slices with a little juice on top and a little drizzling of olive oil.

To serve any leftovers, bring the meat to room temperature, then slice thinly and heat up only the juice. Pour the warm juice over the slices to serve.

STOVETOP PORK IN BALSAMIC VINEGAR

THE
LIST

2 POUNDS 10 OUNCES BONELESS
AND RINDLESS PORK LOIN

5 TABLESPOONS OLIVE OIL

1 TEASPOON BLACK
PEPPERCORNS,
CRUSHED COARSELY

A SPRIG OF SAGE LEAVES
(ABOUT 6 LEAVES)

2 MEDIUM CLOVES GARLIC,
PEELED AND LIGHTLY SQUASHED
WITH THE FLAT OF A KNIFE

¾ CUP BALSAMIC VINEGAR
(A REGULAR ONE WILL DO)

Serves 6

This is my friend Lisa's recipe. Everybody loves it when she makes it and they always say, "There's hardly enough left for panini tomorrow!" And it's true, the leftovers and sauce stuffed into a panino the next day are exceptional. After the long cooking the pork is so tender that it's served more in pieces than slices. I love it with Salt & Pepper Potatoes with a Trickle of Buttermilk (page 110) and a green salad.

Tie up the pork or ask your butcher to tie it for you so it holds its shape neatly. Choose a pot that is not much larger than the pork so the sauce is not too shallow. Pour the oil in and heat well, then brown the pork on all sides, including each end. Salt the browned sides well and turn the pork around in the pot to seal in the salt.

Sprinkle the pepper over all the sides of the pork. Add the sage and garlic to the bottom of the pot and let them fizzle up and give out their flavors. Then, add the balsamic vinegar and let it bubble up. Cover with the lid and turn the heat down to an absolute minimum, hardly bubbling. Use a heat diffuser if you have one. Simmer for 3½ to 4 hours, turning the pork over with tongs every half hour or so and adding just a little water if it looks too dry. The meat is ready when it comes away easily when you pull at it, and when the sauce is glossy and reduced.

Transfer the pork to a chopping board. If the sauce is not abundant, add a little water to the pot and return it to the heat for it to bubble up. Remove the string from the meat, cut it up, and serve with a good amount of sauce.

SAPIENTE
WORDS / PAROLE

AFTER SWEEPING A COLORFUL CARPET,
TAKE A COUPLE OF HEADS OF LETTUCE
AND RUB THEM ALL OVER THE CARPET
TO BRING OUT ITS COLOR.

THE
LIST

1 LONG FLAT PIECE OF
PORK BELLY WITH RIND
(ABOUT 3¼ POUNDS)

1 TABLESPOON OLIVE OIL

3 TABLESPOONS ROSEMARY
& SAGE SALT (PAGE 24)

Serves many

PANCETTA DI MARISA

*A dream. Served warm on two thick slices of white
country-style bread it is wonderful. Bread in Tuscany is
unsalted and it works really well with a very flavorful, fatty
herby meat like this sandwiched in between. Serve it with
something that can stand up to it, such as a radicchio
salad or a plate of cooked bitter greens.*

Preheat the oven to 400°F. Sit a wire rack in a baking pan
so the pork won't touch the bottom of the pan and will
crisp on all sides. Put the pork on a board, skin side up,
and prick the rind here and there with a metal skewer
or sharp-pointed knife—it's quite tough but you will
manage. Turn the pork over and rub the olive oil into the
underside—this will also help the herbed salt stick. Scatter
2 tablespoons of the herbed salt over evenly. Roll up
compactly and tie it with string in three or four places so it
holds its shape. With some oil still on your hands, rub the
skin all over, then rub on the remaining herbed salt.

    Sit the pork on the rack in the pan and drizzle a little
water into the pan. Roast in the oven for about 1 hour
45 minutes, lowering the temperature to 350°F for the last
30 minutes. Drizzle in a little extra water if the bottom of
the pan is threatening to dry out at any point. The outside
of the pork will be deep golden and crispy, and the inside
soft (roast for an extra 10 minutes or so, if necessary).
Serve hot in slices, with bread.

FILETTO IN CROSTA

1 LOAF CIABATTA/
BAGUETTE-TYPE BREAD

2 HEAPING TABLESPOONS
ROSEMARY & SAGE
SALT (PAGE 24)

4 TABLESPOONS OLIVE OIL

1 LONG BONELESS PORK ROAST
(ABOUT 1 POUND 2 OUNCES)

8 SLICES OF LONG PANCETTA

Serves 4 to 6

I love this with Chile & Red Pepper Preserves (page 37) and Salt & Balsamic Vinegar Sautéed Potatoes (page 111). It is best when the meat is just cooked, still a bit rose-colored inside. Choose a loaf of bread of similar size to the pork.

Preheat the oven to 350°F. Halve the bread horizontally. If there is a lot of soft bread under the crusts, pluck out a little. Put most of the herbed salt on a board with 2 tablespoons of the olive oil and rub all over the meat. Heat a nonstick skillet to very hot. Sear the meat on all sides until it's a good color, turning it carefully so you don't burn the herbs. Remove from the pan and nestle it in between the two halves of bread. Scatter with the remaining salt, then close it up like a sandwich and squash it down a bit. Trim away the ends of the bread so the loaf is the same length as the pork. Drape the pancetta over the top and sides. Tie with string in four or five places so the loaf will hold its shape.

 Line a baking sheet with waxed paper. Drizzle another tablespoon of the olive oil onto the bottom. Sit the bread-wrapped roast on top and drizzle with the remaining 2 tablespoons of olive oil. Roast for about 30 minutes, or until it is golden and crusty on top, and when poked with a skewer the meat releases juices that are clear, not pink. Remove from the oven and let sit for 10 minutes or so before slicing into chunky pieces. This is also good at room temperature.

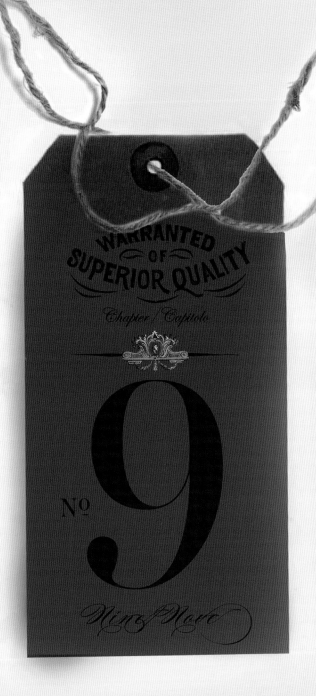

WARRANTED
OF
SUPERIOR QUALITY

Chapter / Capitolo

N⁰ 9

Nine / Nove

— THE —

Dining Room

— FISH —

CHICKPEAS WITH SHRIMP

SEA BREAM WITH FENNEL & POTATOES

PERCH WITH LEMON,
CAPERS & GREEN OLIVE MASHED POTATOES

SHRIMP WITH LARDO & INSALATA DI CAMPO

PEPPER SHRIMP

FISH WITH ESCAROLE, OLIVES & CAPERS

SCORPION FISH WITH ZUCCHINI, CHERRY
TOMATOES & OLIVES

BREAD-CRUMBED BROILED CALAMARI WITH
TABASCO & THYME MAYONNAISE

FISH IN A BOTTLE

SALMON TROUT WITH TARRAGON
SALSA VERDE

BROILED SCALLOPS
WITH TRUFFLE BUTTER

CHICKPEAS
WITH SHRIMP

THE
LIST

10½ OUNCES DRIED
CHICKPEAS, SOAKED
OVERNIGHT IN COLD WATER

3 MEDIUM CLOVES
GARLIC, PEELED, 1 WHOLE
AND 2 CHOPPED

A SPRIG OF SAGE

4 TABLESPOONS OLIVE OIL,
PLUS EXTRA, FOR SERVING

14 OUNCES PEELED RAW
MEDIUM SHRIMP

1 HEAPING TABLESPOON
CHOPPED ROSEMARY

1 (14-OUNCE) CAN
WHOLE TOMATOES

2 GOOD PINCHES OF
CHILI POWDER

LARGE HANDFUL OF ARUGULA

SALT AND FRESHLY
GROUND BLACK PEPPER

Serves 4

*This dish is a lovely, warming mix of rustic and elegant.
Serve it with broiled bread rubbed with garlic and
splashed with olive oil.*

Drain the chickpeas, put in a pot with the whole clove of
garlic and sage, and cover with plenty of cold water. Bring
to a boil. Skim any scum from the surface and cook until
tender, about 50 minutes. They must surrender when you
bite into them. Make sure you have enough water in the
pot at the end, as you will need around 3 cups of cooking
liquid. Add salt only toward the end of cooking. Drain,
keeping the liquid. Take out about a cup of the chickpeas
and keep aside for now. Using a handheld blender, puree
the rest of the chickpeas with about 3 cups of the liquid to
a smooth cream.

Heat 2 tablespoon of oil in a nonstick skillet and add
the shrimp and rosemary. Sauté over high heat until a bit
golden, just a couple of minutes. Scatter a little salt and
pepper on top, transfer to a plate, and keep warm.

Add the remaining 2 tablespoons of oil and the
chopped garlic to the pan. When the garlic starts to smell
good add the tomatoes and chili powder. Season with
salt and a little pepper. Cook over high heat for about 5
minutes, breaking up the tomatoes into big chunks with a
wooden spoon. Pour into the chickpea puree and simmer
together for 5 minutes to meld the flavors.

Spoon the soup into four warm wide bowls and divide
the shrimp among them. Add a few whole chickpeas and
top each with a small handful of arugula. Drizzle with olive
oil, give a grind of pepper, and serve.

SEA BREAM WITH
FENNEL & POTATOES

1¼ POUNDS POTATOES, WASHED

2½ TABLESPOONS OR
SO FENNEL SEEDS

2½ TABLESPOONS
CHOPPED PARSLEY

3 MEDIUM CLOVES GARLIC,
PEELED, 1 CHOPPED
AND 2 WHOLE

2 SMALL SEA BREAM (ORATA,
ABOUT 12 OUNCES EACH),
GUTTED AND SCALED
FOR OVEN ROASTING

2 SPRIGS OF PARSLEY,
WITH STALKS

A LITTLE COARSE SALT

5 TABLESPOONS OLIVE OIL,
PLUS EXTRA, FOR SERVING

2½ TABLESPOONS GRATED
MATURE PECORINO
(OR PARMESAN)

½ CUP WHITE WINE

FRESHLY GROUND
BLACK PEPPER

Serves 2

The fennel here is a beauty. For the sea bream, I like them rounded and small. When I buy fish in Italy they always ask if I want it cleaned for broiling or oven roasting. I like this, that they bother to ask how you will be cooking your fish. I often ask them how to cook it, and for the recipe! Any small whole fish is, of course, suitable.

Cook the potatoes in their skins in boiling salted water until they are soft all the way through, but not falling apart. Drain, and when cool enough to handle, peel them. Slice into rounds of about ½ inch.

Preheat the oven to 350°F. Chop up the fennel seeds, so that some are coarse and some dust. Use a mortar and pestle if you prefer. Set aside. On a small plate, mix the chopped parsley and chopped garlic.

Rinse the fish and wipe with paper towels. Into the cavity of each put a whole clove of garlic, a sprig of parsley and a sprinkle of coarse salt. Drizzle 2½ tablespoons of olive oil into a baking dish that will hold the fish fairly compactly. Lay the potatoes over the oil. Scatter a tablespoon of the garlic parsley, a tablespoon of the pecorino, and a tablespoon of the fennel on top. Salt and pepper the outside of each fish, then lay them on top. Scatter the rest of the garlic parsley, pecorino and fennel over. Drizzle with the last 2½ tablespoons of olive oil on top and pour the wine around, too. Roast, uncovered, for about 30 minutes, or until the fish are roasty looking on top, and when you pierce one in the very middle with a knife, it comes out hot.

Serve the potatoes with the fish, and with a plate on the side to fillet the fish on. Drizzle a little olive oil over the fish on your plate and give a grind of black pepper.

PERCH WITH LEMON, CAPERS & GREEN OLIVE MASHED POTATOES

◇◇

The mashed potatoes are quite abundant, but there is never really enough, is there?

Grate about a teaspoon of zest from the yellow part of the lemon. Keep aside. Cut four slices of lemon, a few fractions of an inch thick, from one end and then squeeze the juice from what's left. Keep aside.

Meanwhile, boil the potatoes in their skins in boiling salted water until they are soft all the way through when you pierce them with a fork. Drain, and when cool enough to handle, peel and then put back in the pot. Mash them, adding the lemon zest. Add the warm milk and butter and turn through well. Stir in the olives and season with salt and pepper. Keep warm.

Heat the oil in a large nonstick skillet, add the garlic and fish fillets, and sauté over medium heat until they are a bit golden underneath. Turn them over, add the lemon slices to the pan, and fry until the fish is golden underneath once more. Turn the lemon slices, too, so they are golden and caramelized on each side. Season with salt and pepper, add the lemon juice, and scatter the capers over the fish. Put on the lid and simmer for a minute more, until the lemon juice is a syrupy sauce and the fish is cooked through. Transfer the fish and lemon slices to warm serving plates. Add ¼ cup of water to the pan and return to the heat. Simmer, uncovered, to reduce a little. Pour over the fish and serve with an extra grind of pepper and a pile of mashed potatoes on the side.

1 LEMON, RINSED AND SCRUBBED

1½ POUNDS POTATOES, SCRUBBED

¾ CUP WARM MILK

3½ TABLESPOONS BUTTER

2½ OUNCES PITTED GREEN OLIVES, HALVED OR QUARTERED IF LARGE

2½ TABLESPOONS OLIVE OIL

2 MEDIUM CLOVES GARLIC, PEELED AND LIGHTLY SQUASHED WITH THE FLAT OF A KNIFE

4 PERCH FILLETS (ABOUT 6 OUNCES EACH)

2 TABLESPOONS SMALL CAPERS IN VINEGAR, DRAINED

SALT AND FRESHLY GROUND BLACK PEPPER

Serves 4

SHRIMP WITH LARDO
& INSALATA DI CAMPO

1 MEDIUM CLOVE GARLIC,
PEELED AND SQUASHED
WITH THE FLAT OF A KNIFE

2½ TABLESPOONS OLIVE OIL

¾ TABLESPOON
BALSAMIC VINEGAR

¾ TABLESPOON LEMON JUICE

1 LARGE MURCOTT MANDARIN
(SEE GLOSSARY, PAGE 328)

2 HANDFULS
INSALATA DI CAMPO/
MISTICANZA (SEE
GLOSSARY, PAGE 328)

6 RAW LARGE SHRIMP,
UNPEELED

6 THIN SLICES OF LARDO
(SEE GLOSSARY, PAGE 328)

2 TABLESPOONS OLIVE OIL

HANDFUL OF THYME SPRIGS,
PLUS EXTRA, TO SERVE,
IF YOU LIKE

2½ TABLESPOONS COGNAC

SALT AND FRESHLY
GROUND BLACK PEPPER

———

Serves 2

Here, shrimp are wrapped in thin, pure white slices of cured pork fat (lardo) and sautéed to give a light savory crust. Lardo di Colonnata was originally a humble food but today it is a prized ingredient in Tuscany. Thinly sliced pancetta could be substituted here. Insalata di campo are wild salad leaves gathered from the fields and they are bitter, beautiful, and quite special.

Make the salad dressing. Put the garlic in a small bowl, add the olive oil, balsamic vinegar, and lemon juice, and season with salt and pepper. Peel the mandarin and cut it crosswise into six slices. Add to the dressing. If the salad leaves are very big, tear them up into good-size pieces.

Peel the shrimp, leaving on the heads and tails. Devein them, then rinse and pat dry with paper towels. Wrap a piece of *lardo* around the body of each shrimp. The loose end will stick. Heat the olive oil in a large nonstick skillet. Carefully add the shrimp in a single layer and sauté over high heat until golden and crusty underneath. Using a pair of tongs, gently turn them over. Add the thyme to the bottom of the pan and sprinkle a little salt and pepper over the shrimp. The *lardo* is well seasoned but you will still need a little. Sauté until golden underneath once more. Standing well back, add the cognac to the pan. It will probably flame up, so take care. When it has burned off, remove the pan from the heat.

Divide the salad leaves between two plates. Drizzle the dressing over the leaves and add the mandarin slices around each salad. Put three shrimp on each plate and drizzle the pan juices on top. Give an extra grind of black pepper and serve at once.

SAPIENTE
WORDS/PAROLE

PEPPERCORNS CAN BE SEWN
INTO LINEN SACHETS AND
KEPT IN POCKETS OF FUR
OR WOOLEN COATS TO KEEP
INSECTS AWAY. THEY CAN ALSO
BE PUT IN JARS OF LENTILS OR
BEANS TO DISTRACT INSECTS.

10 RAW LARGE SHRIMP,
UNPEELED

1 GENEROUS TEASPOON
PINK PEPPERCORNS

1 GENEROUS TEASPOON
BLACK PEPPERCORNS

4 TABLESPOONS OLIVE OIL

2 TABLESPOONS DRIED
BREAD CRUMBS

LEMON WEDGES, TO SERVE

Serves 2

PEPPER SHRIMP

*This is indeed peppery and great. It is good with a
clean-tasting green salad and bread.*

Remove the heads from the shrimp, leaving the shells and
tails intact. Split open down the back to butterfly them,
then devein. Rinse and pat dry with paper towels. Sprinkle
some salt on the cut side of each shrimp.

In a mortar, crush the pink and black peppercorns with
a pestle to break up roughly. Each should be smashed,
some smaller than others. Pour 2½ tablespoons of the
olive oil into an ovenproof dish large enough to take the
shrimp in a single layer. Scatter the bread crumbs over the
bottom, then add the shrimp. Scatter the crushed pepper
over the shrimp. Turn each one over, wiping them in the oil
and bread crumbs, then turn cut side up again and leave
for half an hour or so.

Preheat the broiler to hot. Drizzle the remaining oil over
the shrimp and broil them until opaque and a bit golden
here and there, but not dried out, about 10 minutes. Serve
with a squeeze of lemon juice.

FISH WITH ESCAROLE, OLIVES & CAPERS

1 WHOLE ESCAROLE
(CURLY ENDIVE, ABOUT
1¼ POUNDS)

6 TABLESPOONS OLIVE OIL,
PLUS EXTRA, FOR SERVING

2 MEDIUM CLOVES GARLIC,
PEELED AND SQUASHED
WITH THE FLAT OF A KNIFE

3 ANCHOVY FILLETS, DRAINED

2 TABLESPOONS SMALL
CAPERS IN VINEGAR, DRAINED

ABOUT 12 BLACK OLIVES
(TAGGIASCHE ARE GOOD)

ABOUT 4 TABLESPOONS
ALL-PURPOSE FLOUR

4 FIRM WHITE FISH FILLETS
(ABOUT 6 OUNCES EACH)

4 SAGE LEAVES

ABOUT 1½ TABLESPOON
CHOPPED PARSLEY

¼ CUP WHITE WINE

SALT AND FRESHLY
GROUND BLACK PEPPER

Serves 4

The escarole is also great to serve with Il Bollito (page 209). Try to get a compact escarole that looks like it has been to a neat hairdresser, rather than a wild one.

Rinse the escarole and trim away the bottom. Divide in half lengthwise and then in half crosswise, so you have nice thick chunks. Heat 3 tablespoons of the olive oil in a large nonstick skillet with one clove of garlic and the anchovies, mashing these in with a wooden spoon until they break up and melt into the oil. Add the escarole and cook until wilted, turning it with a pair of tongs so it picks up the flavors in the pan. Add the capers and olives, and season with pepper and a little salt (remember you have anchovies in the sauce). Cook, stirring, on a good heat until much of the water from the escarole has evaporated and you have a thick, chunky heap in the pan, not soggy. Taste for seasoning, transfer to a dish, and keep warm.

Wipe out the pan with paper towels, then heat the remaining 3 tablespoons of olive oil. Pat a little flour over both sides of the fish, shaking off the excess. Panfry the fish until golden underneath. Turn them over using tongs, add the sage and remaining garlic, and panfry until the fish is golden underneath once more. Season with salt and pepper and add the wine to the pan. Cook until the wine has mostly evaporated, then scatter the parsley on top. Serve on a heap of escarole, drizzled with a little extra olive oil and seasoned with lots of black pepper.

SAPIENTE

WORDS/PAROLE

INSIDE A LADY'S HANDBAG IS A COMB,
A NEEDLE AND THREAD, A BAND-AID,
A NATURAL REMEDY, A LIPSTICK—ANYTHING
SHE, A CHILD, OR A MAN MAY NEED. IT'S ALL
THERE AT THE SAME TIME,
TO COVER ALL OF HER CONCERNS.

SCORPION FISH WITH ZUCCHINI, CHERRY TOMATOES & OLIVES

THE
LIST

5 TABLESPOONS OLIVE OIL,
PLUS EXTRA, FOR SERVING

10½ OUNCES SMALL
ZUCCHINI, RINSED AND
SLICED QUITE THINLY

4 FILLETS SCORPION FISH
(ABOUT 1¼ POUNDS TOTAL)

7 OUNCES CHERRY TOMATOES
ON STALKS, BIG ONES
CAN BE HALVED

2 TABLESPOONS
CHOPPED PARSLEY

6 BASIL LEAVES

½ CUP WHITE WINE

20 OR SO WHOLE
BLACK OLIVES

Serves 4

This is lovely and has the accessories (zucchini and tomatoes) included so you don't have to serve any vegetables on the side. All you need to do is the preparation, then it just does its own thing in the oven. You could nip out to the shops—all you need is someone to take it out of the oven for you when the buzzer goes. You can use any delicate white-fleshed fish fillets here.

Preheat the oven to 350°F. I use a rectangular baking dish, about 9 by 13 inches. Drizzle 2½ tablespoons of the olive oil into the dish and scatter the zucchini on top. Salt and pepper both sides of the fish and lay them on the zucchini. Add the tomatoes and scatter in the parsley and torn basil leaves. Add a little salt and pepper over the tomatoes and zucchini. Pour the wine around and throw the olives in. Drizzle the remaining 2½ tablespoons of olive oil on top. Bake for about 30 to 40 minutes, until it's all roasty looking. Serve with a little extra olive oil drizzled over the top.

BREAD-CRUMBED BROILED CALAMARI WITH TABASCO & THYME MAYONNAISE

This can be served as an antipasto or light lunch. Make a couple of crostini from the calamari wings (see below). This is the kind of thing my mother-in-law, Wilma, always does and it adds an extra treat to the meal.

Clean the calamari. This can be done ahead of time and they can be kept them in the fridge until you are ready to eat. Remove the wings and save them for a crostino topping (below). Cut the bodies of the calamari into thick rings about 1¼ inches wide. Leave the tentacles whole unless they are large, in which case halve them. Put the bread crumbs, parsley, and thyme on a plate and mix with some salt and pepper.

Preheat the broiler to the highest temperature. Add the calamari to the crumb mixture and toss them about so they are coated in crumbs. Drizzle 2½ tablespoons of the olive oil over a nonstick baking dish in which the calamari will fit compactly but in a single layer, about 7 by 10 inches. Add the calamari and drizzle the remaining tablespoon of olive oil over the top. Place under the broiler and broil for about 10 minutes, or until the calamari are cooked and the bread crumbs on the bottom of the dish are crusty brown. Serve warm or at room temperature, with lemon wedges and Tabasco & Thyme Mayonnaise.

For the crostini, chop up the calamari wings and sauté in a small skillet with some olive oil until golden. Add some chopped garlic, a little salt and black pepper, and a pinch of chili powder and sauté for a couple of minutes more. Broil two small slices of bread, top with the calamari wings, and drizzle with olive oil.

OLIVE OIL OR ROAST POTATO DROPPED
ONTO A BEAUTIFUL PIECE OF SILK SHOULD
BE IMMEDIATELY DEALT WITH BY SHAKING
TALCUM POWDER ABUNDANTLY OVER THE
MARK TO BLOCK IT. LEAVE UNTIL IT HAS
ABSORBED THE STAIN, THEN SHAKE AWAY.

THE LIST

5 OUNCES LIGHT OLIVE OIL

5 OUNCES SUNFLOWER OIL

1 MEDIUM CLOVE GARLIC,
PEELED AND SQUASHED
WITH THE FLAT OF A KNIFE

2 EGG YOLKS

2½ TABLESPOONS FRESHLY
SQUEEZED LEMON JUICE

1 TEASPOON DIJON MUSTARD

½ TEASPOON CHOPPED THYME

½ TEASPOON CHOPPED PARSLEY

½ TO 1 TEASPOON
TABASCO SAUCE

SALT AND FRESHLY
GROUND BLACK PEPPER

Makes 1¼ cups

TABASCO &
THYME MAYONNAISE

Combine the olive oil, sunflower oil, and garlic in a bowl and leave for 15 minutes or so for the garlic to flavor the oils. Put the egg yolks in a larger bowl and beat with a whisk until creamy. Remove the clove of garlic from the oil and whisk a drop or two of the oil into the egg yolks. When that is amalgamated, whisk in a few drops more. Continue like this until you can see that the emulsion is thickening, then you can gradually increase the rate at which you whisk in the oil. The mixture should become thicker as you go and be quite stiff by the time all the oil has been incorporated. Stir in the lemon juice and mustard. Fold in the thyme and parsley and add salt and freshly ground black pepper to taste. Stir in the Tabasco, to taste.

FISH IN A BOTTLE

4 FIRM WHITE FISH FILLETS
(SUCH AS PERCH OR COD,
ABOUT 5½ OUNCES EACH)

2 SMALL BUNCHES THYME

2 SMALL BUNCHES
PARSLEY, WITH STALKS

10 BLACK PEPPERCORNS

2½ TABLESPOONS OLIVE OIL

2 MEDIUM CLOVES GARLIC,
PEELED AND SQUASHED
WITH THE FLAT OF A KNIFE

DRESSING

5 TABLESPOONS OLIVE OIL

JUICE OF 1 LEMON

1 MEDIUM CLOVE GARLIC,
PEELED AND SQUASHED
WITH THE FLAT OF A KNIFE

SALT AND FRESHLY
GROUND BLACK PEPPER

Serves 4

This is unbelievable. There is no smell of fish in the kitchen or lingering in the house. I imagine a good housewife making this at the same time as she boils other preserves in a water bath. That way she would have preserves prepared for months ahead, and what's more, lunch ready. The house would be smelling of washed sheets and fresh flowers, and she'd be looking as if she's come from the day spa.

You will need two low and wide preserving jars that have good watertight lids. Into each, put two fish fillets, a bunch of thyme and parsley in between, and on top, some salt, peppercorns, a generous tablespoon of olive oil and a clove of garlic. Close and seal the jars well. Place the jars in a wide pot and add enough water to cover at least the necks of the jars (make sure the water won't be able to enter the jars). Take the jars out now and bring the water to a boil. Lower the jars carefully into the boiling water, so they're not touching, and return to a boil. Simmer until the fish turns white, 20 to 30 minutes. Remove the jars from the bath and let cool a little before opening.

While the fish is cooking, make the dressing. Put the olive oil and lemon juice with some salt and pepper in a small bowl and whip until it has thickened a bit. Add the clove of garlic and leave for the flavors to mingle. Serve a fish fillet per plate with some dressing spooned on top. This is so simple, it doesn't need anything else. The little broth collected in the bottles after steaming can be used to dress rice as a first course.

SALMON TROUT
WITH TARRAGON
SALSA VERDE

½ CUP WHITE WINE

1 SMALL WHITE ONION,
PEELED AND HALVED

1 SMALL CELERY STALK

SMALL BUNCH OF PARSLEY

A FEW BLACK PEPPERCORNS

1 SALMON TROUT
(OCEAN TROUT,
ABOUT 1 POUND 14 OUNCES),
FILLETED WITH SKIN LEFT ON

SALSA VERDE (PAGE 18)

SALT AND FRESHLY
GROUND BLACK PEPPER

Serves 2

Lovely, fresh, summery, and easy. Serve with sliced new potatoes boiled in their skins. Don't throw the broth away. Keep it to make a fish risotto later (see below).

Choose a nice wide pot where the fish fillets won't be compromised. Add 1 cup of water, the wine, onion, celery, parsley bunch, peppercorns, and a good pinch of salt and bring to a boil. Clean the fish fillets and remove any bones. Add the fish to the broth, skin side down, cover and simmer for 10 minutes or so. Make sure you splash some of the liquid over the top of the fish. Remove from the heat and leave for about 5 minutes, then carefully transfer each fillet to a plate. Keep the broth to make risotto (see below). Put another plate on top, upside down, and flip it over so it holds the fish, skin side up. Peel the skin away. Flip with the plate-over method once more to have the best side up for presentation. Serve with salsa verde on the side, and boiled new potatoes.

For the risotto, chop ½ small white onion and sauté in 2½ tablespoons olive oil in a wide pan. Add 5½ ounces Arborio or Carnaroli rice (or four fistfuls per person, so eight here). Stir for a couple of minutes, then add some hot water. When it's absorbed, stir in the strained leftover fish broth and simmer for 20 minutes, until the rice is tender.

    To finish, add a generous tablespoon of olive oil and 2 tablespoons of grated Parmesan. Stir in some chopped parsley or any other herb you like. Serve with extra shredded Parmesan and a grind of black pepper.

SAPIENTE
WORDS/PAROLE

BROILED
SCALLOPS WITH
TRUFFLE BUTTER

6 GOOD-LOOKING SCALLOPS
IN THEIR SHELLS

6 HEAPING TEASPOONS
TRUFFLE BUTTER (PAGE 19)

ABOUT 1½ TABLESPOON
DRIED BREAD CRUMBS

SALT AND FRESHLY
GROUND BLACK PEPPER

Serves 2

*One of the easiest recipes I know, and also one
of the most elegant.*

Detach the scallops with their coral from their shells
and rinse and pat dry both. Salt and pepper both sides
of the scallops, then replace them in their shells. Put the
shells on a baking sheet.

Preheat the broiler to high. Spoon 1 heaping
teaspoonful of truffle butter onto each scallop and
sprinkle lightly with bread crumbs. Put under the broiler for
a couple of minutes, until the butter has melted and
the scallops are just cooked through and nicely golden.
Serve at once.

10

— THE —

Sugar Bin

RASPBERRY CARAMEL PASTRIES
WITH CRÈME FRAÎCHE

BRUTTI MA BUONI

LEONTINE'S APPLE CAKE

FRUIT SALAD TART

FILOMENA'S APPLE CAKE

RADICCHIO CAKE WITH WHITE
CHOCOLATE ICING

TORTA TARTUFATA

CHOCOLATE SPREAD

LEMON VERBENA PEACHES & CREAM

ROSE COOKIES

LEMON COOKIES WITH VIOLETS

LAVENDER COOKIES

CROSTATA DI CREMA

CROSTATA WITH PEACH PRESERVES

NONNA'S EGG WHITE CAKE & CANTUCCINI

TORTA CAMPAGNOLA

TORTA MIMOSA

GRANNY JOY'S MARMALADE CAKE

NONNA'S DOLCE DI MARIE

LEMON PIE

BACI DI DAMA

RASPBERRY CARAMEL PASTRIES WITH CRÈME FRAÎCHE

PASTRY

4½ TABLESPOONS BUTTER

½ CUP ALL-PURPOSE FLOUR

4 TEASPOONS SUGAR

CARAMEL SAUCE

4 TABLESPOONS BUTTER

½ TEASPOON VANILLA EXTRACT

⅔ CUP SUGAR

½ CUP HALF-AND-HALF

TO ASSEMBLE

ABOUT 8 HEAPING TEASPOONS
CRÈME FRAÎCHE, NOT
ICE-COLD FROM THE FRIDGE

2 CUPS RASPBERRIES, AT
ROOM TEMPERATURE

CONFECTIONERS' SUGAR,
FOR DUSTING

Makes 8

I love this not-too-sweet combination. You can break up the steps and make the cookies and caramel in advance. The caramel should be taken to a handsome deep cognac color and you can test when it is ready by putting a drop on a white surface. If it looks too light, carry on cooking but take care, as it can burn in a second. This makes eight whispers of a dessert—you may hardly realize you've had dessert.

To make the pastry, cut up the butter into a bowl, then add the flour, sugar, and a pinch of salt and crumble with your fingers to make crumbs. Don't overwork the mixture or it will compromise the cookie texture. Keep the movements of your fingers light and quick. Work in the water to form a soft dough. Gather it into a ball, cover with plastic wrap, and put in the fridge to rest for at least half an hour.

Preheat the oven to 350°F. Line a baking sheet with waxed paper. Remove the pastry from the fridge. Fold one end over the other a few times, pressing down to give a few layers. Divide the pastry into eight portions and use your fingers to flatten each into a disk of 2¾ to 3¼ inches in diameter. Put them on the prepared pan and bake for about 12 minutes, or until pale gold but not too crisp. Remove from the oven and cool. They are fragile, so take care.

For the caramel sauce, gently heat the butter, vanilla, and sugar together in a heavy-bottomed saucepan until melted. Continue cooking over low heat until it is a good amber color. Meanwhile, heat the cream in a separate small saucepan. When the caramel is a good color, carefully whisk in the cream, bit by bit. It will bubble up, so take care. Continue cooking for a minute or so more to ensure that it is smooth and there are no lumps. You may need to give it a good whisk to make it smooth again. If the caramel gets too dark at any point, plunge the pan into a bowl of cold water to stop it from cooking further. Whisk as it cools. Keep, covered, until ready to use. It will be nice and thick, and will cling to your pastry disks.

Take quite a heaping teaspoon of caramel and edge it off onto a pastry disk using another teaspoon. It will spread a bit and settle in. Using the same teaspoon technique, edge a teaspoon or so of crème fraîche over the middle of the caramel and pat out a bit with the spoon to distribute evenly. Set three or four raspberries on top, and put a couple of raspberries on the side. Continue with the other plates in the same way. Shake a little confectioners' sugar over each. You can then turn the raspberries over to see their color. Serve the tarts with a spoon and fork.

BRUTTI MA BUONI

Ugly but good, as the name says. These are often served with coffee, but can be served on their own. I love them with the Coffee & Cinnamon Ice Cream (page 314).

Preheat the oven to 350°F and line two baking sheets with waxed paper. Grind the almonds coarsely so you have a few bits in your cookies. Use electric beaters to whip the egg white and half the sugar to soft peaks in a small bowl first, so you don't have to wash the beaters. Keep aside or in the fridge but don't leave it too long or it will deflate.

Use the electric beaters to whip the butter and the rest of the sugar together until creamy. Add the egg yolk and vanilla, then add the flour, cinnamon, almonds, and a pinch of salt and mix in with a wooden spoon. Fold in the beaten egg white.

Grab chunks of dough smaller than an apricot and rest them on the prepared sheets in rows. Bake for about 12 minutes, until pale golden and firm. Let cool on the sheets and store in a pretty container.

THE
LIST

3½ OUNCES BLANCHED ALMONDS

1 EGG, SEPARATED

⅔ SCANT CUP SUGAR

6½ TABLESPOONS BUTTER, SOFTENED

1 TEASPOON VANILLA EXTRACT

1⅓ CUPS ALL-PURPOSE FLOUR

1 TEASPOON GROUND CINNAMON

SALT

Makes about 28

LEONTINE'S APPLE CAKE

Makes a 9½-inch cake

This is my friend Leontine's cake—everyone is happy when she turns up with it. The crust is great and it lasts well (if there is any left over, that is). It is great alone or with cinnamon cream.

Preheat the oven to 325°F. Butter and flour a 9½-inch round springform cake pan.

Using electric beaters, cream the butter and sugar in a bowl and then beat in the egg. Mix in the flour, baking powder, and vanilla, switching to mix with your hands when it gets too stiff. Knead briefly to incorporate everything.

Put about two-thirds of the dough in the prepared pan. Press it firmly over the bottom and two-thirds of the way up the side. Peel the apples, quarter and core them, and chop into pieces of about ¾ inch. Arrange the apples over the crust and even them out, checking there are no gaps. Crumble the rest of the pastry evenly over the apples in nice big crumbly bits. Bake for 55 to 60 minutes, or until the pastry is golden and firm. Toward the end, cover the top with a sheet of foil if it looks as if it's overbrowning. Remove from the oven and let cool.

Whip the cream to soft peaks, scattering in the cinnamon. Dust the cake with confectioners' sugar and serve with the cinnamon cream.

PASTRY

⅔ CUP BUTTER, SOFTENED

¾ CUP RAW (DEMERARA) SUGAR

1 EGG

½ TEASPOON VANILLA EXTRACT

1⅔ CUPS ALL-PURPOSE FLOUR

½ TEASPOON BAKING POWDER

FILLING

4 CUPS ASSORTED FRUIT, SUCH
AS PEACHES, PEARS, PLUMS,
CHERRIES, STRAWBERRIES,
BLUEBERRIES, NECTARINES

2½ TABLESPOONS RAW
(DEMERARA) SUGAR

CONFECTIONERS' SUGAR,
FOR DUSTING

WHIPPED CREAM, TO SERVE,
IF YOU LIKE

*Makes a 9½-inch cake
+ 10 cookies*

FRUIT SALAD TART

*Here is a lovely fruit tart that is easy to make, and you'll
even have pastry left over to make some sweet and
crunchy cookies (see below).*

Preheat the oven to 350°F. Butter and flour a 9½-inch
round springform cake pan.

To make the pastry, use electric beaters to beat the
butter and sugar together until creamy and pale, about
1 minute. Beat in the egg and vanilla. Mix in the flour and
baking powder. Switching to mix with your hands, knead
quickly to incorporate everything. Put aside one-third
of the dough (about 5½ ounces) to make the cookies.
Press the two-thirds of dough firmly onto the bottom and
two-thirds of the way up the side of the prepared pan.

For the filling, prepare the fruit—halve strawberries and
cherries if large, remove pits and slice stone fruit, and cut
other large fruit into big chunky slices. Put in a bowl and
sprinkle with the 2½ tablespoons of raw sugar. Stir gently.
Distribute the fruit evenly over the crust. Bake for about 50
minutes, or until the fruit looks lovely and jammy, trapped
in a cage of pastry. Remove from the oven and let cool.
Dust with confectioners' sugar and serve in slices, alone or
with whipped cream.

COOKIES

Bake these while you finish the tart. Break off ten pieces of
the reserved dough, each about the size of a walnut, and
roll in your palms. Flatten slightly. Place on a baking sheet
lined with waxed paper, leaving space for spreading. With
the dough that's left, make decorations such as initials
and put on top of the cookies. Bake for 10 minutes or so,
until golden. Offer as treats or snacks.

FILOMENA'S APPLE CAKE

11 TABLESPOONS
BUTTER, SOFTENED

¾ CUP SUGAR, PLUS 2½
TABLESPOONS, EXTRA

2 TEASPOONS VANILLA EXTRACT

3 EGGS, SEPARATED

1²/₃ CUPS ALL-PURPOSE FLOUR

2½ TABLESPOONS
POTATO FLOUR

2 TEASPOONS BAKING POWDER

4 TABLESPOONS MILK

3 RENNET APPLES
(OR OTHER LARGE SWEET
COOKING APPLES; SEE
GLOSSARY, PAGE 329),
(ABOUT 7¾ OUNCES EACH)

CONFECTIONERS' SUGAR,
FOR DUSTING

Makes a 9¹/₂-inch cake

This is somewhere between a cake and a tart. It is my friend Marta's mother's recipe. When I made it and took it to Marta, I could see she was nicely surprised by my effort. It's quite fun when you make someone's own recipe and take it to them! Anyway, Marta was adamant that next time I use rennet apples as I had used whatever I could get that day. She said, "No, no, no. Tttt, ttt, ttt. Rennet."'

Preheat the oven to 325°F. Butter and flour a 9½-inch round springform cake pan.

Using electric beaters, whip the butter and ¾ cup of the sugar in a wide bowl until creamy. Add the vanilla, then add the egg yolks one at a time, whisking well after each. Whisk in the flour, potato flour, and baking powder, adding the milk as the mixture thickens to make it come together in a very thick batter. Scrape the mixture off the beaters into the bowl, then wash and dry them. Use the clean beaters to whip the egg whites to snowy peaks. Using a metal spoon, fold a scoop of the egg whites into the cake batter until evenly dispersed, then gently fold in the rest of the whites. If they are difficult to incorporate, give a quick whisk with the electric beaters to mix it all together. Scrape into the prepared pan and level the surface.

Peel, core, and halve the apples. Cut across the halves into slices of ⅛- to-¼-inch. Starting at the center of the cake, arrange the slices slightly obliquely, pushed about halfway into the batter. Pack them tightly together, working your way outward, like the petals of a rose. It may seem as if there is too much apple, but fill in any spaces as it will look lovely later. Scatter the extra 2½ tablespoons of sugar evenly over the top. Bake until the apples begin to get golden and some of the edges are dark, about 45 minutes, then cover with foil and continue baking for a further 15 to 20 minutes, or until the cake is done. (The middle should look ever-so-faintly gooey.) It is important that the cake is not overcooked, as the edges and bottom will dry out.

Remove the foil and let cool before removing from the pan. Serve dusted lightly with confectioners' sugar.

RADICCHIO CAKE WITH WHITE CHOCOLATE ICING

◇◇

1 GENEROUS TABLESPOON
DRIED BREAD CRUMBS

2½ TABLESPOONS SUGAR,
PLUS ½ CUP EXTRA

5½ OUNCES TRIMMED
ROUND RADICCHIO (HALF
OF A SMALL ONE)

7 TABLESPOONS
BUTTER, SOFTENED

3 EGGS

1 TEASPOON FINELY
GRATED LEMON ZEST,
YELLOW PART ONLY

1 GENEROUS TABLESPOON
BRANDY

1 TEASPOON
VANILLA EXTRACT

A GOOD GRATING
OF NUTMEG

1 CUP ALL-PURPOSE FLOUR

2 TEASPOONS
BAKING POWDER

SALT

WHITE CHOCOLATE ICING

5½ OUNCES WHITE
CHOCOLATE, CHOPPED

Makes an 8-inch cake

This is my sister-in-law Luisa's recipe. It comes from Chioggia, where they have lots of radicchio. It is surprisingly good with a lovely texture, and it keeps well.

Preheat the oven to 350°F. Butter an 8-inch round springform cake pan. Scatter in the bread crumbs and shake it so the bread crumbs stick to the butter. Shake out the excess.

Bring 4 cups of water to a boil with the 2½ tablespoons of sugar. Loosen the radicchio leaves and add to the boiling water. Cook for a few minutes to soften. Drain and pat dry with paper towels, then chop up.

Using electric beaters, whip the butter with the extra ½ cup of sugar until creamy. Whip the eggs in one by one, then add the lemon rind, brandy, vanilla, and nutmeg, whisking in to blend. Add the flour, baking powder, and a pinch of salt, whisking until smooth. Fold in the cooled radicchio. Scrape the mixture into the prepared pan and bake for about 40 minutes, or until a skewer inserted in the center comes out clean. Remove from the oven and let cool completely before removing from the pan.

For the icing, melt the chocolate in a bain-marie (see Glossary, page 328). When it has cooled a little and begun to thicken, spread it thickly over the top of the cake.

TORTA TARTUFATA

1½ OUNCES HAZELNUTS,
SKINNED

7 TABLESPOONS BUTTER

4¼ OUNCES DARK
UNSWEETENED
CHOCOLATE, CHOPPED

2½ TABLESPOONS
UNSWEETENED COCOA
POWDER

3 EGGS, SEPARATED

½ CUP SUGAR

½ TEASPOON
VANILLA EXTRACT

2½ TABLESPOONS
+ 2 TEASPOONS
ALL-PURPOSE FLOUR

CONFECTIONERS' SUGAR,
FOR DUSTING

SALT

Makes an 11¼-inch cake

This is Marzia's recipe. She adores baking and is always honored to give out her recipes. This is a nice, flat chocolate cake. Easy to make, easy to eat. Its name is truffle cake because it is chocolatey and moist.

Preheat the oven to 350°F. Butter and flour an 11¼-inch round springform cake pan. Toast the hazelnuts in a dry frying pan just enough to draw out their flavor. Coarsely chop the nuts, leaving good texture.

   Melt the butter in a saucepan and add the chocolate and cocoa. Stir until the chocolate has melted and is smooth, then remove from the heat. Leave to cool. Using electric beaters, whip the egg whites in a bowl to snowy peaks, then keep aside for now. Use the electric beaters to whip the egg yolks, sugar, and vanilla in a generous, wide bowl until creamy. Stir in the chocolate mixture. Next, whisk in the flour, nuts, and a pinch of salt. Finally, gently fold in the creamy egg whites with a metal spoon, folding from the bottom to the top as though you are drawing circles with the spoon in the batter.

   Scrape out into the prepared pan and bake for about 20 minutes, or until the top looks like dry desert soil, but the middle is still moist and soft. Let cool before serving with a light dusting of confectioners' sugar.

CHOCOLATE SPREAD

4½ TABLESPOONS BUTTER

5 TABLESPOONS MILK

4¼ OUNCES DARK
UNSWEETENED
CHOCOLATE, CHOPPED

⅓ CUP SUGAR

Makes just under 1 cup

This is a simple chocolate spread you can put on bread. It's also great on a just-cooked plain pizza base, scattered with toasted hazelnuts (see Sweet Pizza, page 61).

Set up a bain-marie (see Glossary, page 328). Put the butter, milk and chocolate in the bowl. When it starts melting add the sugar, stirring until it is thick and smooth. Let cool. It will keep in a closed jar in a cool place for about 10 days.

LEMON VERBENA
PEACHES & CREAM

¼ CUP SUGAR

1 GENEROUS
TABLESPOON HONEY

4 WHITE PEACHES
(WITH RED STREAKS,
ABOUT 1¼ POUNDS TOTAL)

5 GENEROUS SPRIGS
(4 INCHES LONG OR SO EACH)
FRESH LEMON VERBENA,
PLUS EXTRA, TO SERVE,
IF YOU LIKE

MASCARPONE CREAM

¾ CUP HEAVY WHIPPING CREAM

5½ OUNCES MASCARPONE

2 TEASPOONS
CONFECTIONERS' SUGAR

A FEW DROPS OF
VANILLA EXTRACT

Serves 4

This is beautiful and refreshing. It's worth growing lemon verbena in your garden for its incredible smell alone. Before it dries up for the winter I collect and dry as many leaves as I can and then I can't wait for summer again. I always drink it as a tea with a little honey.

Here, I have poached peaches in a lemon verbena infusion. The peaches I love are white with tinges of red in their skin and through their flesh. This gives a beautiful color to the syrup. If you can't get these peaches, add a couple of raspberries to the poaching liquid.

Put the sugar, 2 cups of water, and the honey in a pot just big enough to take the peaches side by side. Bring to a boil, then reduce the heat to a simmer and add the whole peaches. If necessary, top up the water level to just cover the peaches (but not so much that the syrup will be diluted). Tuck in the lemon verbena. Tear off a square of waxed paper larger than the diameter of your pot and press it down onto the tops of the peaches. Simmer gently (rapid boiling may cause the fruit to break up) until poached but still firm and holding their shape well, about 8 minutes.

Transfer the peaches to a flat bowl to cool for a bit. When they're cool enough to handle, slip off the skins—they should come away like silk dresses. If not, return them to their bath to simmer a while longer. Leave the syrup in the pot to cool.

Meanwhile, make the mascarpone cream. In a small bowl, gradually mix together the cream and mascarpone. Add the confectioners' sugar and vanilla, and beat until smooth.

Serve a cooled peach in a flat bowl with syrup and a good spoonful of mascarpone cream.

SAPIENTE

WORDS/PAROLE

IF SOMETHING IS WORTH DOING,
IT'S WORTH DOING WELL

THE
LIST

ROSE COOKIES

5½ TABLESPOONS
BUTTER, SOFTENED

⅓ CUP + 2 TABLESPOONS
SUGAR, PLUS A LITTLE
EXTRA, FOR SPRINKLING

1 EGG

A FEW DROPS OF
VANILLA EXTRACT

1 TEASPOON ROSE WATER

1²/₃ CUPS ALL-PURPOSE FLOUR

TINY FRESH UNSPRAYED
ROSEBUDS OR ONES YOU
HAVE DRIED (SEE PAGE 282),
HALVED LENGTHWISE

ABOUT 1 TEASPOON
GUM ARABIC, IF USING
DRIED ROSEBUDS (SEE
GLOSSARY, PAGE 328)

Makes 15

These are true beauties. You can set fresh rosebuds on them before baking or stick dried ones on top after baking. You can also fold dried rose petals into some of the dough before shaping the cookies for a variation (these wouldn't need a rosebud on top). The rosebuds are edible, but you might prefer to pick them off before eating.

Preheat the oven to 325°F and line a baking sheet with waxed paper. Using electric beaters, cream the butter and sugar together until pale and thick. Beat in the egg, then add the vanilla and rose water. Add the flour and mix in with a wooden spoon. You can keep the dough in the fridge or make the cookies immediately.

Break off balls of dough the size of a rum ball, just a little more than 1 tablespoon. Roll them into smooth balls with your hands. Flatten them ever so slightly, then place on the lined sheet, leaving a little space between each. Use a plastic bottle cap (from a bottle of water, for example) to gently press a ring pattern on the top of each cookie.

If using fresh rosebuds, set a half bud on top of each cookie, pressing it in gently. Sprinkle a little extra sugar over the top. Bake for 10 minutes, until just set but still very pale (they will harden as they cool). Transfer them to a wire rack to cool.

If using dried rosebuds, you can put them on now. Mix a little gum arabic with enough water to give a sticky paste. Using a toothpick, put a few drops on the outside of a rosebud and press it gently onto the cookies.

DRYING ROSEBUDS
& VIOLETS

Gather tiny unsprayed rosebuds and violets that have no dew or water on them. Spread on a tray and put in a dry, sunny spot indoors; for example, in front of a window. Leave until completely dried, turning them over now and then, and opening out any petals that may have curled in. Violets will be ready in a matter of days, but rosebuds will need longer.

LEMON COOKIES
WITH VIOLETS

THE
LIST

5½ TABLESPOONS
BUTTER, SOFTENED

⅓ CUP + 2 TABLESPOONS
SUGAR, PLUS A LITTLE
EXTRA, FOR SPRINKLING

1 EGG

A FEW DROPS OF
VANILLA EXTRACT

½ TEASPOON GRATED
LEMON ZEST, YELLOW
PART ONLY

1⅔ CUPS ALL-PURPOSE FLOUR

ABOUT 1 TEASPOON
GUM ARABIC (SEE
GLOSSARY, PAGE 328)

ABOUT 20 DRIED
UNSPRAYED VIOLETS

Makes 20

Preheat the oven to 325°F and line a baking sheet with waxed paper. Using electric beaters, cream the butter and sugar together until pale and thick. Beat in the egg, then add the vanilla and lemon zest. Add the flour and mix in with a wooden spoon. You can keep the dough in the fridge or make the cookies immediately.

Break off balls of dough the size of a rum ball, just a little more than a tablespoon each. Roll them into smooth balls with your hands. Flatten them ever so slightly, then place on the lined sheet, leaving a little space between each. Sprinkle a good pinch of sugar over the tops. Use a plastic bottle cap (from a bottle of water, for example) to gently press a ring pattern on top of each cookie. This gives them a nice shape when baked. Bake for 10 minutes, until just set but still very pale (they will harden as they cool). Transfer them to a wire rack to cool.

Mix a little gum arabic with enough water to give a sticky paste. Using a toothpick, put a few drops on the underside of a violet and press gently onto a cookie.

SAPIENTE

WORDS/PAROLE

A PLACE FOR EVERYTHING AND
EVERYTHING IN ITS PLACE

LAVENDER COOKIES

THE
LIST

5½ TABLESPOONS
BUTTER, SOFTENED

⅓ CUP + 2 TABLESPOONS
LAVENDER SUGAR (PAGE 42)

1 EGG

A FEW DROPS OF
VANILLA EXTRACT

1⅔ CUPS ALL-PURPOSE FLOUR

ABOUT 20 FRESH UNSPRAYED
LAVENDER FLOWER TIPS

SUGAR, FOR
SPRINKLING

Makes 20

Preheat the oven to 325°F and line a baking sheets with waxed paper. Put the butter and lavender sugar in a bowl and use electric beaters to beat well, until a little pale and the sugar has dissolved, about 30 seconds. Beat in the egg and vanilla. Add the flour and mix in with a wooden spoon. Keep the dough in the fridge or make the cookies immediately.

Break off balls of dough the size of a rum ball, a little more than a tablespoon each. Roll them into smooth balls with your hands, then flatten them a bit. Place on the lined sheet and press a lavender tip gently onto the top of each. Sprinkle with a little sugar and bake for about 10 minutes, until just set but still very pale (they will harden as they cool). Transfer them to a wire rack to cool.

CROSTATA DI CREMA

I like this plain, sometimes with a raspberry put in each window while it is still warm. You can brush a little of the unused egg whites over the pastry before baking, then put the rest toward Nonna's Egg White Cake (page 289).

To make the *crema*, in a heavy-bottomed pot whip the egg yolks, sugar, and vanilla until thick and creamy. Whip in the flour until smooth. Add a little of the milk to amalgamate, then whip in the rest of the milk and the cream. Add the lemon zest. Put over low heat and bring to a very gentle boil, whisking all the time until it thickens. Remove from the heat and let it cool, whisking every now and then to prevent lumps from forming.

Preheat the oven to 325°F. Butter a round 9½-inch round springform cake pan.

To make the pastry, put the flour and a pinch of salt in a bowl. Rub the butter in well with your fingertips. Add the egg yolk, whole egg, and sugar and knead lightly until it all comes together. Roll out two-thirds of the pastry into a disk, roughly 12 inches in diameter. Ease the pastry into the pan, to cover the bottom and come about halfway up the side. Divide the remaining third of pastry into twelve portions and roll these on a lightly floured surface into thin ropes of varying lengths.

Plop the cooled *crema* into the middle of the pastry case and spread out lightly with a spatula. Lay the pastry ropes over, half going one way and half crosshatching the other way. Trim the ends and neaten the sides. Brush the pastry lightly with egg white, using a narrow brush. Bake for 35 to 40 minutes or until the pastry is golden and crisp. Let cool, then dust with confectioners' sugar and serve in slices.

CROSTATA
WITH PEACH PRESERVES

**7 TABLESPOONS
BUTTER, SOFTENED**

2⅓ CUPS ALL-PURPOSE FLOUR

¾ CUP + 2 TABLESPOONS SUGAR

2 EGGS, LIGHTLY BEATEN

**½ TEASPOON BAKING
POWDER**

**14 OUNCES PEACH PRESERVES
(PAGE 39) OR OTHER PRESERVES**

**1 EGG YOLK, WHISKED,
FOR GLAZING**

Makes an 11¼-inch tart

This is delicious and quick to make. Use your favorite jam—it looks super with a red jam, too. I like to make two of these with different color preserves and serve a slice of each. You can use a little milk to brush over the pastry if you don't want to use up an egg yolk, but the yolk will give you a glossier and deeper color.

Put the butter in a bowl with the flour, sugar, eggs, baking powder, and a pinch of salt and mix together well. Knead the dough into a compact ball, flatten a bit, and wrap in plastic wrap. Chill in the fridge for half an hour or so.

Preheat the oven to 350°F. Butter an 11¼-inch round loose-based tart pan.

Break off one-third or so of the pastry and keep to one side. On a large sheet of waxed paper, roll out the larger piece of dough into a circle of about 13½ inches, as it needs to go up and above the side of the pan. Using the waxed paper as a tray, position it over the pan and then flip it so the pastry is underneath. Quickly ease it into the pan and peel away the waxed paper. Work the pastry over the base and up the side of the pan, pressing it gently into place. Prick the bottom here and there with a fork. Spoon the preserves in and spread them to cover the pastry evenly. Turn the sides of the pastry down over the jam to neaten.

Roll the remaining third of dough into eighteen ropes of various lengths to cover the tart in a crisscross diamond pattern. Lay them in place, then trim the ends. Using a small brush, brush the pastry with the whisked egg yolk. Bake for 25 to 30 minutes, or until the pastry is deep golden and the bottom crisp. Let cool before slicing. This keeps well, covered, for a few days.

NONNA'S EGG WHITE CAKE

This is what Nonna does to use up egg whites after using the yolks in a cream or elsewhere. It is lovely as a cake, but quite special turned into Cantuccini (see below).

4 EGG WHITES

¾ CUP SUGAR

7 TABLESPOONS
BUTTER, MELTED

1 TEASPOON
VANILLA EXTRACT

1 TEASPOON FINELY
GRATED LEMON ZEST,
YELLOW PART ONLY

⅔ CUP ALL-PURPOSE FLOUR

1 TEASPOON BAKING POWDER

½ CUP GROUND ALMONDS

¼ SCANT CUP POTATO FLOUR

Makes a 9½-inch cake

Preheat the oven to 325°F. Butter a round 9½-inch round springform cake pan and line the base with waxed paper.

Using electric beaters, first whisk the egg whites in a bowl until white and snowy. Keep aside. Without washing the beaters, whisk the sugar, butter, and vanilla in a separate bowl until the sugar has dissolved. Use a wooden spoon to mix in the lemon zest and then the flour, baking powder, ground almonds, potato flour, and a pinch of salt. The mixture will be very stiff.

Using a metal spoon, fold one-third of the egg whites into the mixture until evenly dispersed, then gently fold in the rest of the whites. If they are difficult to incorporate, give a quick whisk with the electric beaters to mix it all in. Spoon the mixture into the prepared pan and bake for 25 to 30 minutes, or until springy and a skewer inserted in the middle comes out clean. Let cool.

CANTUCCINI

Preheat the oven to 235°F and line a baking sheet with waxed paper. Slice right across the cake to make strips ⅝-inch thick. Cut these into two or three long lengths and lay on their sides on the lined tray. Bake until dry and golden, about 40 minutes. Remove from the oven and let cool on the tray. Store in a cookie container, where they will keep for many weeks.

TORTA CAMPAGNOLA

*Simple, feathery light, and wonderful for breakfast.
Or anytime, really. The kind of cake your grandmother
would have made.*

Preheat the oven to 350°F. Butter and flour a 9½-inch
round springform cake pan.

Whip the egg whites to snowy peaks in a bowl first so
you don't have to wash the beaters. In another bowl, use
the beaters to whip the egg yolks, sugar, lemon zest and
juice, vanilla, and olive oil until creamy. Add the milk and
mix in well to blend. Beat in the flour and baking powder.

Fold in the beaten egg whites and scrape out into
the prepared pan. Bake for about 30 to 35 minutes, until
beautiful, golden, and risen, and a skewer inserted in the
middle comes out clean. It will probably have a nice crack
across the top.

TORTA MIMOSA

*The mimosa flower is a symbol of the strength and
love of women. In Italy, on the Festa della Donna on the
8th of March it is common to give a few sprigs of the
bright yellow blossoms to female friends, colleagues, or
anyone special to you. Torta mimosa is abundant at this
time of year. Use eggs with very yellow yolks for the best
color. The cake can be made a day ahead and assembled
on the day of serving.*

Preheat the oven to 350°F. Butter and flour a 9½-inch
round springform cake pan.

To make the cake, use electric beaters to whip the egg
whites to snowy peaks. In a separate bowl, whip the egg
yolks, sugar, and vanilla. Combine the flour, potato flour,
and baking powder and whisk into the yolk mixture. Fold
in a scoop of egg whites and when that is combined, fold
in the rest. Scoop the mixture into the prepared pan, level

CREMA

2 CUPS MILK

A FEW DROPS OF
VANILLA EXTRACT

SMALL STRIP OF LEMON
ZEST, YELLOW PART ONLY

4 EGG YOLKS

½ CUP SUGAR

3 TABLESPOONS
ALL-PURPOSE FLOUR

½ CUP HEAVY WHIPPING CREAM

2½ TABLESPOONS
BOUGHT OR HOMEMADE
LIMONCELLO (PAGE 17)

the surface and bake for about 30 minutes or until golden and a skewer inserted in the center comes out clean. Let cool in the tin for 10 minutes, then turn out onto a wire rack and let cool completely.

To make the *crema*, heat the milk, vanilla, and lemon zest in a medium saucepan to just below boiling. Use electric beaters to cream the egg yolks and sugar in a bowl. When they are pale and thick, mix in the flour. Whisk a little of the near-boiling milk into the egg mixture and then add the rest, whisking all the time. Now pour it all back into the saucepan and cook over low heat, stirring, until the mixture is thick and smooth. Take off the heat and let cool completely, stirring often as it cools.

Whip the cream to stiff peaks. Remove the lemon zest from the *crema* and fold the whipped cream through.

Slice the cake in half horizontally. Carefully pluck out the center of the cut side of each half, ¼ to ½ inch deep and leaving a border of about ½ inch. Reserve the part you've taken out. Splash the *limoncello* evenly over the cut sides. Put the bottom half of the cake on a large flat plate, cut side up. Spoon two-thirds of the *crema* into the center and spread evenly, then position the top half of the cake in place. Spread the rest of the *crema* over the top and sides of the cake.

Use your fingers to crumble the reserved cake into fairly uniform bits that look like mimosa blossoms. Scatter them over the top and sides of the cake, pressing them gently onto the *crema* to stick. Cover the cake as evenly as you can. The cake is now ready to serve. It will keep well in a cake pan in a cool spot for a couple of days.

SAPIENTE
WORDS/PAROLE

THE CHILDREN OF MY CHILDREN
ARE TWICE MY CHILDREN.

GRANNY JOY'S MARMALADE CAKE

THE
LIST

13 TABLESPOONS
BUTTER, SOFTENED

¾ CUP + 2 TABLESPOONS SUGAR

3 EGGS

1 TEASPOON VANILLA
EXTRACT

8 TABLESPOONS ORANGE
MARMALADE

1 TABLESPOON GRATED
ORANGE ZEST, ORANGE
PART ONLY

1⅓ HEAPING CUPS
ALL-PURPOSE FLOUR

1½ TEASPOONS
BAKING POWDER

GLAZE

2 TABLESPOONS ORANGE JUICE

½ CUP CONFECTIONERS' SUGAR

Makes a 9½-inch cake

Use homemade (page 38) or bought orange marmalade here. You can have this lovely cake for afternoon tea or you might like to serve it after a meal with a little whipped cream on the side.

Preheat the oven to 350°F. Butter and flour a 9½-inch round springform cake pan or, if you prefer, a Bundt pan.

Using electric beaters, cream the butter and sugar together in a mixing bowl. Add the eggs one by one, beating well after each. Add the vanilla, marmalade, and orange zest. Beat in the flour and baking powder.

Scrape out into the prepared pan and bake for about 40 minutes, until golden and set. Test with a knitting needle—stick it in the center of the cake and if it comes out clean, the cake is done. Let cool before turning out and drizzling with the glaze.

To make the glaze, stir the orange juice into the confectioners' sugar until dissolved and smooth.

NONNA'S DOLCE DI MARIE

¾ CUP SUGAR

½ CUPS STRONG ESPRESSO
COFFEE, COOLED

14 TABLESPOONS
BUTTER, SOFTENED

10½ OUNCES RECTANGULAR
MARIE (PETIT BEURRE) COOKIES

1 OUNCES DARK UNSWEETENED
CHOCOLATE, GRATED

ABOUT 1 TEASPOON
GROUND COFFEE BEANS

Serves quite a few

I was surprised when various friends told me of this cake that their nonnas made. And when I made it, I was surprised to find everyone still likes it, even if they haven't had it for years. It would have been the kind of thing that was thrown together with simple ingredients always on hand. It reminds me of the Marie cookies we used to have as children—one with a layer of butter, another with a layer of jam, and sandwiched together.

Add 1 heaping tablespoon of the sugar to the espresso coffee and stir until it dissolves. Pour into a flat bowl. Using electric beaters, cream the remaining sugar and the butter together until smooth and pale.

You will need a rectangular dish close to 10 by 7 inches. Start with a single layer of cookies. Dip the cookies one by one in the coffee, making sure they are bathed on both sides but not so much that they go soggy or fall apart. Lay them on the bottom of the dish to completely cover it. Spatula one-quarter of the butter cream over, spreading it evenly. Next, scatter one-quarter of the chocolate over the top. Take a pinch of the ground coffee and scatter that over the chocolate.

Repeat the procession three more times, finishing with a final scattering of chocolate and ground coffee. Your work is done. Put it in the fridge for an hour or two before cutting off a small square for a snack. It's rather rich, so you judge how big you want the squares to be.

SAPIENTE

WORDS/PAROLE

IF LIFE GIVES YOU LEMONS,
MAKE LEMON PIE.

LEMON PIE

9 TABLESPOONS
BUTTER, CHOPPED

4½ OUNCES RECTANGULAR
MARIE (PETIT BEURRE)
OR GRAHAM CRACKERS

1 CUP HEAVY WHIPPING CREAM

1 (12-OUNCE) CAN
CONDENSED MILK

JUICE OF 2 LARGE LEMONS

Serves a family

This is my sister Ludi's recipe. She can make it with her eyes closed. It has a nice, old-fashioned atmosphere to it. I get the feeling the original recipe must have come from the back of a condensed milk can years ago. Whatever the case may be, it's lemon heaven. It is as easy as it can get to make a pie, though it needs a good few hours to set and hold in the fridge, so making it the day before is perfect. You can scatter a handful of chopped almonds over the top if you like, or just serve it plain.

Put the butter in an 8½ by 6¼-inch heatproof ceramic or glass dish and put it in the sun or on the stovetop to melt. Crush the cookies in a food processor or blender. Add to the butter and mix well. Press firmly and evenly onto the base of the dish.

Whip the cream until fairly stiff. Add the condensed milk and whip to incorporate. Now for the magic—quickly whisk in the lemon juice and see how the mixture thickens! Scrape out over the cookie base and level the surface. Cover the dish with plastic wrap and refrigerate until set. When ready to serve, take the dish from the fridge and cut into not very big, loose squares. If the base seems too firm to cut, leave it at room temperature for 10 minutes or so and then cut.

BACI DI DAMA

6¼ OUNCES BLANCHED
ALMONDS

¾ CUP, PLUS
2 TABLESPOONS SUGAR

13 TABLESPOONS BUTTER,
AT ROOM TEMPERATURE

1⅓ CUPS
ALL-PURPOSE FLOUR

ABOUT 3½ OUNCES DARK
UNSWEETENED
CHOCOLATE

Makes about 35

Also known as lady's or dame's kisses. Many places in Italy have these wonderfully crisp cookies, sandwiched together with a layer of dark chocolate. What could possibly be wrong with that?

Toast the nuts lightly in a dry skillet, taking care not to burn them. Let cool a bit, then grind with a tablespoon or so of the sugar. Cream the remaining sugar and butter, using electric beaters. Add the flour and then the nuts, mixing by hand now to incorporate. Put in the fridge for a while so the dough is easier to work with.

Preheat the oven to 325°F. Line two baking sheets with waxed paper.

Break off balls of dough the size of a cherry, about ½ tablespoon each. Put them on the prepared sheets, leaving a little space between each for spreading. Bake for about 20 minutes, until pale gold. Remove and cool.

Meanwhile, melt the chocolate in a bain-marie (see Glossary, page 328). Stir until smooth, then remove from the heat and let cool a little but don't let it set again. Using a teaspoon, dab some melted chocolate (not so much that it oozes out) on the bottom of a cookie and grab a partner for it. Gently press the two together. Continue until all the couples are taken. Put them on a wire rack to set and stay together, and then you can move them to a pretty lined tray or a lovely container.

— THE —

Ice Box

BACI DI SIENA

MASCARPONE & LAVENDER ICE CREAM
WITH WILD STRAWBERRIES

GRANITA DI MANDORLE

PAN BRIOCHE

COFFEE & CINNAMON ICE CREAM

GIANDUIA ICE CREAM MATTONE
WITH WHIPPED CREAM

MILK & MINT ICE CREAM

LIMONCELLO SORBET

FIOR DI LATTE ICE CREAM

One

THERE SEEMS TO
BE A SECRET CODE
AMONG WOMEN. AN
UNSPOKEN GUARANTEE
THAT WILL BREAK
SILENCES. HOLD
THINGS UP. LET YOU
STEP OVER BARRIERS,
CROSS BOUNDARIES
TO COLLECT THINGS.
RECIPES. A RECIPE
IS THE SECRET CODE
THAT ALLOWS YOU
TO SHARE SPACE AND
TIME WITH ANOTHER IN
THE LINE AT THE

THE ICE BOX

BUTCHER, BAKER, OR
CANDLESTICK MAKER.
LIKE A GIFT TO BE
PASSED ON.

+ *Truth* +
+ **LOVE** +
& *Honor*

No. 118.

♥

Two

MANY WOMEN
CONSIDER IT PRECIOUS
KNOWLEDGE THAT
MUST BE PASSED ON
FROM WOMAN TO
WOMAN AND BE SAVED.
THEIR MISSION IS TO
PRACTISE THE ART AND
PASS IT ON. THIS CODE
SEEMS TO UNITE MOST
WOMEN. AND FOR
A WOMAN A RECIPE IS
LIKE A TROPHY. THIS
IS HER WAY. HER BEST
SALSA. HER BEST CAKE.

♥ THE ICE BOX ♥

THAT DESERVES AN
AWARD. WHEN WE HEAR
OF AN OLDER WOMAN
WHO IS A GREAT COOK,
SHE COMMANDS
RESPECT. SHE IS
A SUPERWOMAN.
A TROPHY TAKER.

No. 118.
♥

SAPIENTE

WORDS/PAROLE

TO A VALIANT HEART,
NOTHING IS IMPOSSIBLE.

THE
LIST

1 CUP HEAVY WHIPPING CREAM

14 OUNCES DARK
UNSWEETENED CHOCOLATE

3½ OUNCES HARD NOUGAT,
COARSELY CHOPPED

2 TABLESPOONS
OLIVE OIL

———

Makes about 10

BACI DI SIENA

I love finding this kind of thing in the freezer, and evidently so does everyone else, because whenever I make them and go back to get more there are none. Each will make one rich portion or they can be shared.

Whip the cream stiffly, as it has to hold all the other ingredients. Chop ¾ ounces or so of the chocolate into bits. Add to the cream, along with the nougat, and fold in. Line a tray with waxed paper that will fit in your freezer. Scoop up 1 generous tablespoon of the cream and use another tablespoon to edge it off onto the waxed paper to form a small hill. When all the cream has been used, put the tray in the freezer for about an hour to set the hills.

Melt the remaining chocolate in a bain-marie (see Glossary, page 328), stirring with a wooden spoon. Remove from the heat, stir in the olive oil and let cool a little. It needs to be liquid, but not hot, for dipping. When the hills are frozen, drop them one at a time into the chocolate and turn them over, using 2 tablespoons, to coat completely on all sides. Set them back on the tray and return to the freezer to set the chocolate. Once set, wrap them up in foil and tie with a ribbon. Keep in the freezer and serve directly from there.

MASCARPONE & LAVENDER ICE CREAM WITH WILD STRAWBERRIES

1 CUP MILK

1 HEAPING TEASPOON
UNSPRAYED LAVENDER FLOWERS

3 EGG YOLKS

½ CUP SUGAR

1 TEASPOON VANILLA EXTRACT

9 OUNCES MASCARPONE

A SMALL CUPPED HANDFUL
OF WILD STRAWBERRIES
PER PERSON, TO SERVE

Serves 6 to 8

This ice cream freshens you up, leaving a gentle hint of lavender lingering on. You can use fresh or dried lavender. Fresh lavender flowers should be collected in branches at the end of summer, then left to dry in bunches. I love this with wild strawberries when they are in season. You can keep the egg whites toward another use such as Nonna's Egg White Cake (page 289) or they can be stored in the freezer, with a label to remind you how many there are.

Put the milk in a medium pot and bring slowly to a boil. Add the lavender flowers just before it boils and then take the pot off the heat. Leave for about 10 minutes to infuse, stirring so the lavender perfumes the milk.

Use electric beaters to beat the egg yolks, sugar, and vanilla in a medium bowl until pale, thick, and creamy. Strain the perfumed milk into the egg mixture, whisking to incorporate so the eggs don't curdle. Return all the mixture to the pan and cook over low heat until slightly thickened. It is important to use a very low heat and whisk for just a short time so the eggs don't curdle. Set aside to cool for 5 to 10 minutes, stirring every now and then.

Whisk in the mascarpone until free of lumps, then let cool completely. Churn in an ice-cream machine, following the manufacturer's instructions. Alternatively, pour into a shallow tray and put in the freezer. When it is just frozen, after about 1 hour, beat vigorously with a fork to break up the ice crystals and then return the tray to the freezer. Repeat this process twice before leaving it to freeze completely. Keep in the freezer in a sealed container.

If the ice cream seems too hard to serve initially, leave it at room temperature to soften slightly. Serve scoops of the ice cream with some wild strawberries.

Rose

Il profumo dei fiori

GRANITA DI MANDORLE

9 OUNCES BLANCHED ALMONDS

⅔ CUP SUGAR

Makes 2½ to 3 cups

This is adored in Sicily, especially as breakfast in summer. Every day. Some even make it in winter. Can't get tired of it, they say. In fact, many Sicilians even have a special machine for this into which they toss ice, sugar, and almonds and out comes an ice-white beauty. To get it to the same consistency as I ate it with the Sicilians, you will need an ice-cream machine to whip subtlety and life into it. Serve for breakfast with Pan Brioche (opposite).

Put the almonds in a dry skillet and toast gently until they just start to color, turning them almost continuously. Watch that they don't darken, as this will change the milky white color of the granita. Remove from the heat and let cool completely.

Blend the almonds, sugar, and roughly a cup of water in a food processor until you have a smooth paste. Add 2 more cups of water and blend. Line a colander with muslin and set it over a deep bowl. Scrape the almond mixture into the colander and put aside, covered loosely, to drain overnight.

Remove the colander and, holding the almond–filled muslin over the bowl, twist and squeeze it firmly (taking care not to tear the fabric) to get the last of the milk from the pulp. You should have just under 3 cups of almond milk. Now stir in 2 or 3 tablespoons of the almond pulp, depending on how much texture you like. You won't need the remaining pulp, so you can discard it. Pour the milk into an ice-cream machine and churn, following the manufacturer's instructions.

Once frozen, store in a suitable container in the freezer and take it out a little before serving so it makes nice soft dollops in a cup, not hard scoops.

PAN BRIOCHE

¼ OUNCE FRESH YEAST OR 2
TEASPOONS ACTIVE DRY YEAST

3 TABLESPOONS
TEPID MILK

2 EGG YOLKS, PLUS 1 EXTRA,
FOR BRUSHING

3⅓ CUPS ALL-PURPOSE FLOUR

5 TABLESPOONS
BUTTER, MELTED

½ CUP SUGAR

1 TEASPOON
VANILLA EXTRACT

1 TEASPOON ORANGE
FLOWER WATER

SALT

———

Makes 9

The beauty of these rolls is in their lightness. My Sicilian friend insists they must be served with almond granita. They need to be made the night before, then left to rise, punched down, left to rise for a further 4 hours, shaped, and left to rise once more before baking.

In a large bowl, crumble or place the yeast into the milk and leave for a few minutes, until bubbly. Add the two egg yolks and the flour, butter, sugar, vanilla and orange flower water along with a pinch of salt. Mix to a soft dough, adding a little more flour or tepid milk as necessary. Knead on a lightly floured work surface until smooth and springy, about 5 minutes. Return to the bowl, cover with plastic wrap and then a cloth, and leave in a warm spot to rise overnight.

Next morning, punch down the dough. Cover again and leave to rise in a warm place for about 4 hours, after which the dough will be very light and puffy. Line two baking sheet with waxed paper—they need to be sheets with sides so you can put a cloth over the rising dough without it touching the dough. Punch down the dough again. Form into nine oval-shaped rolls. Lay them on the sheets now, as you won't be able to move them after they have risen. Leave, covered, until well puffed up.

Meanwhile, preheat the oven to 350°F. Whip the extra egg yolk and gently brush over the tops of the brioches with a pastry brush. Take care as they can easily deflate if you prod them too roughly. Bake for about 15 minutes, until pale gold. Transfer to a wire rack to cool. Break off large pieces and scoop into Granita di Mandorle (opposite). On their own they are great with butter and preserves, plain or toasted.

2 CUPS HEAVY WHIPPING CREAM

1 STICK OF CINNAMON

1 TEASPOON
VANILLA EXTRACT

1 TEASPOON UNSWEETENED
COCOA POWDER

4 EGGS

2/3 SCANT CUP SUGAR

1 CUP STRONG
ESPRESSO COFFEE

Serves 8 to 10

COFFEE &
CINNAMON ICE CREAM

*I like to serve this with Brutti Ma Buoni (page 268)
or sometimes with a blob of whipped cream on top.
I use a "moka" coffee maker to make a strong coffee (see
Glossary, page 329).*

Heat the cream, cinnamon stick, vanilla, and cocoa powder in a large saucepan. Using electric beaters, whisk the eggs and sugar in a bowl until thick and pale.

When the cream is just coming to a boil, stir in the coffee. Whisking constantly so nothing scrambles, slowly pour the cream and coffee mixture into the sugary eggs. Scrape it all back into the pan and return to a very low heat, whisking with a hand whisk to thicken slightly and cook the eggs. Take care not to scramble them.

When it is ready (it should coat the back of a spoon), remove from the heat and whisk regularly until it cools completely. Remove the cinnamon stick. Pour into an ice-cream machine and churn, following the manufacturer's instructions. Alternatively, pour into a shallow tray and put in the freezer. When it is just frozen, after about 1 hour, beat vigorously with a fork to break up the ice crystals and then return the tray to the freezer. Repeat this process twice before leaving the ice cream to freeze completely. Store in the freezer in a sealed container.

GIANDUIA
ICE CREAM MATTONE
WITH WHIPPED CREAM

3½ OUNCES HAZELNUTS,
SKINNED

2 CUPS MILK

8½ OUNCES DARK
UNSWEETENED
CHOCOLATE, CHOPPED

5 TABLESPOONS DARK
UNSWEETENED
COCOA POWDER

4 WHOLE EGGS

¾ CUP SUGAR

1 TEASPOON
VANILLA EXTRACT

1 CUP HEAVY WHIPPING CREAM

UNSWEETENED WHIPPED
CREAM, TO SERVE

Serves 6 to 8

*This is a chocolatey brick of ice cream topped with
a pile of whipped cream. Quite delicious!*

Line a 9½ by 3¼-inch loaf pan with plastic wrap or waxed
paper, leaving some overhang to make it easier to remove
the ice cream. Toast 1½ ounces of the hazelnuts lightly
in a dry skillet, then chop them by hand to small bits. Put
aside. Heat the milk in a large saucepan, then add the
chocolate, stirring every now and then. When melted, stir
in the cocoa and beat until smooth. Remove from the
heat.

In a medium bowl, whisk the eggs with the sugar,
vanilla, and a pinch of salt until pale and creamy. Slowly
drizzle in some hot chocolate mixture, whisking so it
doesn't scramble. When all the chocolate is incorporated,
pour the mixture back into the pan, add the chopped
hazelnuts to infuse, and put over very low heat. Whisking
all the time, heat for a couple of minutes to cook out the
eggs. There's no need to thicken. Remove from the heat
and let cool, whisking now and then.

Whisk in the cream, then cool in the fridge until well
chilled. Strain the mixture directly into the prepared pan,
and discard the hazelnuts. Put in the freezer to set.

Halve some of the remaining hazelnuts and quarter
the rest. Toast them all in a dry skillet with a light sprinkle
of salt, then leave to cool. To serve the ice cream, unmold
and cut into chunky slices. Serve one or two slices with
dollops of whipped cream and some toasted hazelnuts
scattered on top.

Altro che niagra,
hij em quella
loup.... tutt'a
tro che nispati,
eg.!

SAPIENTE
WORDS/PAROLE

MEASURE TWICE
CUT ONCE

MILK & MINT
ICE CREAM

2 CUPS MILK

½ CUP SUGAR

ABOUT 16 MINT LEAVES

1 CUP HEAVY WHIPPING CREAM

Serves 6 to 8

This ice cream is delicate and subtle, and very easy to eat. It's nice with a small cookie, a square of dark chocolate or just on its own.

Heat the milk and sugar in a saucepan. Just as the milk is coming to a boil, toss in the mint and then remove from the heat. Leave it to infuse and cool down completely.

Remove the mint leaves with a slotted spoon and whisk in the cream. Pour into an ice-cream machine and churn, following the manufacturer's instructions. Alternatively, pour into a shallow tray and put in the freezer. When it is just frozen, after about 1 hour, beat vigorously with a fork to break up the ice crystals and then return the tray to the freezer. Repeat this process twice before leaving the ice cream to freeze completely. Store in the freezer in a sealed container.

TO LOOK AFTER YOUR BRUSHES,
WASH THEM IN MILK, THEN
RINSE IN WARM WATER AND LET
THEM DRY IN THE SUN.

LIMONCELLO SORBET

1 LONG STRIP OF
LEMON ZEST,
YELLOW PART ONLY

1 SCANT CUP SUGAR

JUICE OF 3 LEMONS
(ABOUT 5 OUNCES)

3 TABLESPOONS
BOUGHT OR HOMEMADE
LIMONCELLO (PAGE 17)

Makes just over 2 cups

*Serve this with Fior di Latte ice cream (opposite).
I love the combination of lemon and fior di latte.*

Put 1 cup of water, the lemon zest and sugar in a pot.
Bring to a boil, then reduce the heat and simmer for 5
minutes. Remove from the heat. Stir in the lemon juice
and the *limoncello*. Let cool completely. Remove the strip
of lemon zest. Churn in an ice-cream machine, following
the manufacturer's instructions. Store in the freezer
in a sealed container.

FIOR DI LATTE ICE CREAM

1 CUP MILK

A FEW DROPS OF
VANILLA EXTRACT

½ CUP SUGAR

1 CUP HEAVY WHIPPING CREAM

Makes just over 2 cups

Fior di latte *is probably my favorite flavor in ice cream. Just milky cream. It always takes its partner to its best potential, and even alone is like a breath of fresh air.*

Heat the milk in a pot with the vanilla and sugar, stirring until the sugar has dissolved. Remove from the heat and stir in the cream. Leave to cool completely. Churn in an ice-cream machine, following the manufacturer's instructions. Alternatively, pour into a shallow tray and put in the freezer. When it is just frozen, after about 1 hour, beat vigorously with a fork to break up the ice crystals and then return the tray to the freezer. Repeat this process twice before leaving the ice cream to freeze completely. Store in the freezer in a sealed container.

SAPIENTE

WORDS/PAROLE

MY MOTHER ALWAYS SAID: NEVER RUN
AFTER A MAN OR A BUS—THERE IS
ALWAYS ANOTHER ONE COMING.

Glossary

AGRETTI, also known as roscano or saltwort, is a grasslike spring vegetable from northern Italy that can often been found growing wild by salty marshes. It has a crisp, grassy freshness and is slightly tart and a bit salty.

ACACIA *(Robinia pseudoacaci)* is a legume with pods and is edible, unlike its cousin mimosa. The acacias found in Europe are a different species to the thorny acacias of Australia and Africa.

BAIN-MARIE is a water bath used to gently heat ingredients. In this book it is used to melt chocolate, by putting the chocolate in a heatproof bowl over a saucepan of simmering water. The base of the bowl must not come in contact with the water, in order for the chocolate to melt without immediately setting again.

BURRATA is a rich, fresh, cow's milk cheese, similar in taste and appearance to a very creamy fresh mozzarella.

BUTTER used in Tuscany is most commonly unsalted. If you use salted butter to make these recipes be mindful of this when seasoning them.

CARDOONS, known as *cardi* in Italian, are a member of the thistle family. The stalks are eaten either raw when young or blanched, braised, or baked when older and tougher. Celery may be substituted.

CAVOLO NERO, literally meaning "black cabbage", has loose, very dark green leaves with stalks. Other types of kale or savoy cabbage may be substituted.

CHICKENS are often sold with their heads and legs attached from Italian butchers.

FLOUR in Italy is graded according to its gluten content or "hard" qualities. The most commonly available are 0 (strong/bread flour) and 00, which is used for cakes and patisserie. However, there's a lot of contention about which type is best for what. I prefer hard flour for breads.

GUM ARABIC is sometimes known as acacia gum or Senegal gum. It is edible in small amounts and is tasteless, odourless, and water-soluble so it makes a good adhesive for culinary uses, such as attaching decorations to cakes or cookies.

HIMALAYAN SALT has pink and clear crystals, and comes from salt mines in Pakistan. It contains no preservatives or additives and is high in natural minerals.

INSALATA DI CAMPO/MISTICANZA translates literally as "salad from the field" and is generally a mixture of fairly bitter leaves, such as various radicchio, endive, tops of wild fennel and flower tops, that varies with the seasons.

LARDO used in Tuscany is *lardo di Colonnata*, which originated around the Carrara marble mines. Cured with herbs (mainly rosemary) and spices, it is a pure white, soft rendered pork fat with a sweet smooth flavor. It is often used for wrapping foods before cooking, and thinly sliced pancetta may be substituted. It is also enjoyed on broiled or plain bread.

LAVENDER that is used for culinary purposes needs to be the edible variety, *lavandula augustafolia*, which is also known as true lavender, English lavender, and lavender vera. Other varieties are not palatable and give an unpleasant soapy taste to foods.

MANITOBA FLOUR is obtained by milling varieties of hard wheat grown in North America, originally Manitoba in Canada. It forms a very high quantity of gluten during the kneading and cooking of bread.

MOKA COFFEE MAKER is the stove-top *caffetiera* loved by all Italians, who will have several machines of different sizes lined up on their kitchen shelf.

MURCOTT MANDARIN is a cultivar of tangerine that is sometimes called honey or honey murcott. It has a thin rind and strong flavor, and is very juicy. It can also have a lot of seeds. Any variety of mandarin may be substituted.

PORCINI MUSHROOMS are also known as cepes or boletus, and are available from late summer into autumn in cooler regions. The thick white stem holds much of the flavor. When using fresh porcini, the stems need to be cooked for longer than the fleshy caps.

RED BULB SCALLIONS have elongated, deep purple-red bodies and a mild sweet flavor. Shallots may be substituted.

RENNET APPLES are an old French variety, also called reinette, with firm, dry flesh, a strong flavor, and long keeping, all of which make them ideal for cooking. Fuji apples may be substituted.

SALSICCIA is sausage, and can mean either fresh sausage, as in pork sausages, or cured, such as salamis. In this book, the *salsiccia* used is always fresh.

CHILES in Italy generally come from the sunny Italian south and are quite mild in flavor.

STRACCHINO is a rindless, fresh cow's milk cheese that has a mild fresh taste.

VALERIANA is wild lamb's lettuce, also known as corn salad and mâche. Watercress that has been picked over could be substituted.

ZIBBIBO RAISINS are small, seedless dark raisins from the muscat grape.

Preserving and sterilizing

PRESERVING

Whenever you are preserving foods, the ingredients should be as fresh as possible. Pack the fruit or vegetables into jars, seal with the lids, and then process (bring to a boil and boil for at least 20 minutes) in the sealed jars. If the ingredients are not to be processed, any air bubbles should be removed by pushing the ingredients down with a fork. They should then always remain covered with their preserving liquid (oil, vinegar, syrup and so on).

When making preserves, I have learned from my mother-in-law to spoon the hot preserves into the clean sterilized jars, close the lids tightly, and turn the jars upside down. They are left there, covered with a tea towel to cool completely. This creates a vacuum that can be seen on the lid, ensuring no air remains in the jars. The jars can then be stored upright in a cool, dark place for a few months. While it is safer to boil the jars, this is a quick and effective method. However, the time they will last depends on the amount of sugar you have used, as it acts as preserving agent, so take special care when little sugar is used.

Use small, rather than large, jars for preserves as they can be used up quickly once opened. The tops or lids used should always be new and fit tightly. The jars should be kept in a cool, dark place until they are opened. After this, store them in the refrigerator and consume quickly. Clean cutlery should always be used when extracting the contents of the jars.

Homemade preserves that are not preserved in vinegar or salt and have no preservatives are more susceptible to bacteria as they lack the acidity that blocks their development. Take extra care with preserved foods to avoid botulism, a type of food poisoning caused by toxins from *Clostridium botulinum* bacteria. The bacteria can be present in tiny quantities and is very hard to detect, so if the contents of a jar ever look or smell suspicious, you should discard it.

STERILIZING

To sterilize glass jars, wash them thoroughly in hot soapy water and then rinse under hot water. Place on a baking sheet and put in an oven preheated to 235°F until the jars are completely dry. Leave them in the oven until you are ready to fill them.

The
INDEX

Acknowledgments

Thank you to my team: photographer Manos, stylist Michail and
art director Lisa for your talent, endless creativity and inspiration.
To my sister-in-law Luisa and to Jo, my food editor, thanks for
your incredible help and support.
Thank you to Riccardo Barthel, for your generosity in letting
us in to your beautiful space (my FAVORITE shop in Florence).
Thank you to David for creating the possibility, and Caterina
for the beautiful fabrics.

Thank you, Lisa McG, for your valuable support always.
To Mom, Ludi, Dad, Nin, Artemis, Leontine, Anabelle, Anjalika,
Barbara, Diana, Ketty, Julietta, Giovanna, Lucia, Laura, Matteo,
Ioanna, Joanna, Sylvia, Luisa, Paolo, Cetina, Lidia, Mariella, Marzia,
Olga, Marisa, Marta, Filomena, Pierluigi, Emily, Peta, Patrizia,
Rebecca, Jan, Carmella, Claudia, Nicci, Roberto, Filippo, Massimo,
Gianluca, Carlos, Trong, Jackie - thank you all for your recipes
and the many other gracious ways you have helped.
Thank you to all at Murdoch. To my publishers, Sally and Chris -
thank you for your trust. And to my editor Anna, to Livia, Deborah
and the many others involved in making this book - thank you for
your hard work.
Thank you, Giovanni, Yasmine and Cassia, my precious family -
for your patience, your encouragement.
To Mario - thank you for sharing your knowledge and for all
these beautiful photographs you took of Wilma.
And finalmente, Wilma - thank you for all you have given.

Andrews McMeel Publishing, LLC
an Andrews McMeel Universal company
1130 Walnut Street, Kansas City, Missouri 64106

www.andrewsmcmeel.com

Published in 2012 by Murdoch Books Pty Limited
Pier 8/9, 23 Hickson Road, Millers Point, NSW 2000

Text © Tessa Kiros 2012
The moral right of the author has been asserted.
Design © Murdoch Books Pty Limited 2012
Photography © Manos Chatzikonstantis 2012

12 13 14 15 16 MUB 10 9 8 7 6 5 4 3 2 1

ISBN: 978-1-4494-2521-0

Library of Congress Control Number: 2012936738

Publisher: Sally Webb
Design concept: Lisa Greenberg
Design coordination: Robert Polmear
Photographer: Manos Chatzikonstantis
Stylist: Michail Touros
Food Editor: Jo Glynn
Editor: Anna Scobie
Project Manager: Livia Caiazzo
Production Manager: Karen Small

OVEN VARIATION: You may find cooking times vary depending on the oven you are using.
For fan-forced ovens, as a general rule, set the oven temperature to 35°F lower than
indicated in the recipe.